Marketing Campaign Development

What marketing executives need to know about architecting global integrated marketing campaigns

By Mike Gospe

20660 Stevens Creek Blvd.
Suite 210
Cupertino, CA 95014

Marketing Campaign Development:
What marketing executives need to know about
architecting global integrated marketing campaigns

First Printing: March 1, 2008
Paperback ISBN: 1-60005-077-8 (978-1-60005-077-0)
Place of Publication: Silicon Valley, California, USA
Paperback Library of Congress Number: 2007939873

eBook ISBN: 1-60005-078-6 (978-1-60005-078-7)

Trademarks

Warning and Disclaimer

Endorsements for Marketing Campaign Development

"Mike's approach to integrated marketing and his use of program blueprints are the tools that will keep the spirit of the guerrilla marketer alive."
Jay Conrad Levinson, The Father of Guerrilla Marketing, with over 15 million copies sold

"Mike has written a great inspirational 'how to' book for business-to-business marketers in the Internet age. His examples and prescriptions really got my creative juices flowing! He shows you how to focus, align and motivate your executives, your distributed marketing professionals, your publicists, and your sales organization (direct and indirect channels). He explains how you can design holistic, integrated marketing campaigns that address the specific needs of individual customers in particular roles in targeted industries. This is customer-led marketing at its best!"
Patricia B. Seybold, Author, Outside Innovation, The Customer Revolution, and Customers.com

"A true 'marketing process' approach that aligns customers, sales and marketing for marketplace success. Practical and powerful."
Don Schultz, Professor, Northwestern University, and author of the book 'Integrated Marketing Communications'

Dedication

To Mary,

Sean,

and Zachary

for

your support

and

encouragement.

Acknowledgements

Necessity, they say, is the mother of invention. The same is true for this book. Because I couldn't find a recipe for working cross-functionally to develop a truly integrated marketing campaign, I had to invent one.

My quest began in 1985 when I was a young ambitious marketer working for Hewlett-Packard. If I have achieved success in this book it is because I had plenty of help along the way. In truth, so many people have contributed so extensively to my learning over the years that it is no longer possible to say precisely to whom I am indebted—except for three notable exceptions. I am greatly indebted to Cindy Kennaugh and Elaine Miller, two of the very finest marketing strategists and politically-savvy campaign leaders I have ever known and had the pleasure to work with. And I wish to thank Brian Gentile, a friend and colleague who is a continuing inspiration for me to be the best marketing leader I can be.

Without family and friends, the formation of this book wouldn't have been possible. I thank my KickStart Alliance team of Mary Gospe, Mary Sullivan, and Janet Gregory for their constant inspiration and editorial assistance. Special thanks also go to Sridhar Ramanathan, Tobey Fitch, and Susan Thomas for their tutelage. And I offer my sincere appreciation to Mitchell Levy, my publisher, for his unending support.

A Message From Happy About®

Thank you for your purchase of this Happy About book. It is available online at http://happyabout.info/marketingcampaigndevelopment.php or at other online and physical bookstores.

- Please contact us for quantity discounts at sales@happyabout.info
- If you want to be informed by e-mail of upcoming Happy About® books, please e-mail bookupdate@happyabout.info

Happy About is interested in you if you are an author who would like to submit a non-fiction book proposal or a corporation that would like to have a book written for you. Please contact us by e-mail editorial@happyabout.info or phone (1-408-257-3000).

Other available Happy About books include:

- 42 Rules of Marketing:
  http://happyabout.info/42rules/marketing.php
- Scrappy Project Managment:
  http://happyabout.info/scrappyabout/project-management.php
- Expert Product Management:
  http://happyabout.info/expertproductmanagement.php
- Awakening Social Responsibility:
  http://happyabout.info/csr.php
- I'm on Facebook--Now What???:
  http://happyabout.info/facebook.php
- I'm on LinkedIn--Now What???:
  http://happyabout.info/linkedinhelp.php
- Tales From the Networking Community:
  http://happyabout.info/networking-community.php
- Happy About Online Networking:
  http://happyabout.info/onlinenetworking.php
- Foolosophy:
  http://happyabout.info/foolosophy.php
- Climbing the Ladder of Business Intelligence:
  http://happyabout.info/climbing-ladder.php
- The Business Rule Revolution:
  http://happyabout.info/business-rule-revolution.php
- Happy About Joint Venturing:
  http://happyabout.info/jointventuring.php
- The Home Run Hitter's Guide to Fundraising:
  http://happyabout.info/homerun-fundraising.php

Contents

Contents

Figures

While many of us will recognize a good, well-thought-out marketing campaign when we see one, the single, basic truth about world-class marketing campaign development is that it is easy to say, but hard to do. It is hard to do because we all like to take short-cuts. I hear the lament all too often: "I'm over-worked and don't have the time to think strategically," or "Planning is overrated. I just need to get these projects done." As a result, we take short-cuts like "Ready, fire, aim." Lack of planning is the slippery slope that leads to wasteful marketing. Then one day we get the call from the corner office to come and explain why our marketing efforts did not produce the desired results.

Luckily, developing world-class marketing campaigns is achievable for any marketing team. Successful marketing requires following a disciplined, systematic approach to working cross-functionally and cross-regionally in order to prioritize marketing objectives, design a customer-engaging go-to-market strategy, and execute the plan. This book is your guide. It will show you how to optimize your marketing efforts and achieve an even greater return on your marketing investment.

I've been there. I know. For more than 20 years I've worked the angles of campaign management. I've led a team of go-to-market strategists at Hewlett-Packard, guided a worldwide organization to tailor global strategies for regional application at Sun, and coordinated a team of corporate marketing experts to execute specific campaigns at Ariba. I've experienced the euphoria of designing marketing campaigns that produced wildly successful response rates. And, I've earned battle scars with campaigns that were a disaster. In each case, I paid attention to noting why some worked and others didn't. Over the years I've collected and shared campaign development best practices with companies, clients, and colleagues. The result of this research is now captured in this book.

This book is not about marketing theory. It's a practical, pragmatic "how to" book designed for hi-tech marketing leaders, as well as corporate, regional, and marketing operations managers at every level. If you play a role in the development and execution of marketing campaigns, this book is for you.

This unique book takes you step-by-step through the disciplined, yet practical, process of architecting truly integrated marketing communications plans that work. In it, you will find a prescription for building a successful, repeatable campaign development process, including the necessary templates and helpful, practical techniques. The templates are also available online at:

www.kickstartall.com/campaign_development.html

Good luck and good selling!

1 The Truth about Campaign Development

In this chapter we describe what campaign development is and what it is not. We'll also define key terms and set some expectations for the results that companies can receive by embracing these best practices.

"In order to improve your game, you must study the endgame before everything else, for whereas the endings can be studied and mastered by themselves, the middle game and the opening must be studied in relation to the endgame." [1]

Jose Raul Capablanca—one of the world's first chess grandmasters

Why is campaign development important?

Good marketing can be equated to playing chess. Chess grandmasters are winners because they have been trained to think several moves ahead. And in this planning they are able to react to their

---

1. Chess-poster.com, http://tinyurl.com/qfaqm

opponents' moves with skill and finesse. They study the situation, making note of possible moves and then follow-on moves. They anticipate reactions, and then act accordingly. This very same approach is what separates the best marketing campaigns from the rest.

In 1990 the Washington Post ran an article about the increasing level of noise in the marketplace.[2] In those pre-Internet days, they estimated that the average person, you and I, received more than 3,000 messages from companies every day. To make matters worse, 99% of these messages were irrelevant to the people who heard them. These messages bombarded us from the moment we woke up to the sound of the alarm clock radio. They hammered at us through newspapers, magazines, billboards. They echoed through word-of-mouth, television, even product placements in movies. In total, the result was three thousand drummers trying to get our attention. Then along came the Internet. Some estimates place today's noise level at more than 10,000 messages every day.

What does this mean to us marketers? It means that we must take extra care to make sure that every message we communicate and every marketing vehicle we choose is relevant and meaningful to our target audience. It's not about mass marketing any more. It's not even about niche marketing. It's about promoting a personal dialog via one-on-one marketing techniques that speak to the needs of prospects and customers, anticipate their reactions, and get results.

> **The world is our chess board; the marketing vehicles are our chess pieces.**

We must fight the temptation of blasting irrelevant messages to large groups of people and instead become relevant to our target audiences. We can only hope to achieve success if we are thoughtful and pay attention to what we are saying, and when and how we are delivering the message. Success today requires marketers to apply the discipline of campaign development to better our chances of being able to cut through the clutter and be heard. This is how we will win marketing's chess game.

---

2. Washington Post, Ads: They're Everywhere! By Paula Span, April 28, 1990, page c.01.

Sun Microsystems: a case study

In January 1997, I worked for Sun as one of its first marketing strategists and campaign managers. After careful investigation of the trends driving what would become the dotcom boom, we concluded that:

1. 75% of all servers running the Internet were running the Sun Solaris operating system, and
2. Nobody knew it.

Back in 1997, Sun was most commonly recognized as the provider of technical workstations. CEO Scott McNealy saw an opportunity to become more: for Sun to become the "Internet foundation." The first step in changing the rules was not to invent a new product, but to change the way Sun talked about itself and marketed its solutions. To achieve this positioning shift, Sun embarked on a two-phased marketing campaign that would first create awareness of Sun as the backbone of the Internet and then reposition Sun as a thought leader on business requirements for leveraging the Internet.

But this new marketing campaign wouldn't just magically appear. It would require a new customer-centric process for developing a marketing campaign. This was a significant change from the product-focused campaigns of the past. Sun's executive team took the following action:

- **Formation of a new team:** Instead of the usual product-focused marketing teams dictating marketing tactics, they anointed a virtual cross-functional, cross-geography marketing team that would be held accountable for architecting and executing an awareness campaign. The goal of this new type of campaign was to put Sun in a thought leadership position regarding "all things Internet."

- **Goals made visible:** McNealy, with management support at every level, introduced this team and its goals to the rest of Sun.

- **Introduction of the campaign manager:** The vice president of global marketing introduced the role of the campaign manager, a new role within Sun, to guide the effort to unite/support a worldwide marketing team.

- **Timeline defined:** Competitive threats were many, and the window of opportunity was narrow. This team was given 90 days to develop the marketing strategy and a tactical plan for phase 1.

This new process gave birth to Sun's first truly integrated global marketing campaign. It was called the WebTone campaign. The word "WebTone" was defined to be "the 21st century Internet equivalent to today's dialtone." McNealy described this concept at every opportunity.

"In today's world, people pick up a phone, hear a dial tone, then communicate instantaneously around the world—in fact, you "boot" your telephone by just picking it up. Some companies are already taking advantage of a computing network without technologic, geographic or time barriers—a network over which partners, customers and employees can collaborate at any time, from anywhere, with anyone. To gain that competitive advantage, businesses are turning to the Internet, and Sun is providing the network foundation and delivering the continuous WebTone that makes it all possible."

Scott McNealy [3]

The campaign development team understood that success would not be achieved overnight. Changing market perception would take 18 months to two years. It became immediately clear that their first challenge was to avoid the temptation to execute tactics for the sake of executing tactics. There were hundreds of marketing activities that could be performed. Everyone had his or her pet project. But throwing marketing efforts and dollars at everything would have been like tossing lit matches into the wind hoping one created a fire, burned brightly, and got noticed.

To ignite success that was worthy of attention with press and analysts as well as prospects and customers, the team knew they had to **prioritize and understand their target audiences first**. Only then

---

3. Businesswire, "Sun reveals software strategy for establishing "WebTone" future of computing; Leading the charge to Java-ready information-efficient networks," April 15, 1997

would they be able to craft a story that would capture interest and speak to the relevance and opportunity that Internet computing provided. The first questions that needed to be answered included:

1. Who are our primary target audiences and what are their business pain points?
2. How can we help them gain competitive advantage using the Internet more than any competitive alternative?
3. What is the most effective way of engaging with these audiences to tell them our story and nurture a dialog with them?

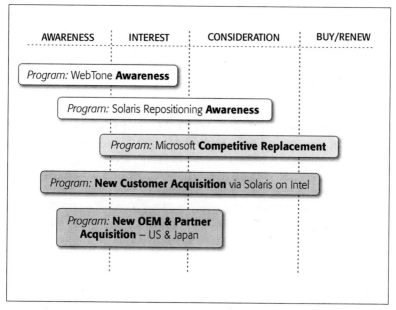

Figure 1: Sun's WebTone Marketing Campaign Map

After careful consideration and analysis, the team put forth a strategy to break the WebTone campaign into two phases. The first phase was focused on establishing awareness and credibility for Sun in the Internet space. Five marketing programs were selected that, when concurrently executed, would show that Sun had the business expertise as well as the technological expertise to truly be a leader in this space (see Figure 1).

With the campaign strategy now identified and agreed upon, marketing creativity blossomed. Comprised within each of these five supporting programs was a small, but carefully scoped, series of marketing activities. Some of these were routine, others were not. Traditional marketing activities included: print and radio advertising that built on itself (like chapters in a book) over nine months; a new website and collateral materials; tightly-knitted sales messaging and training. But, creativity took a leap forward with the pursuit of new activities that had never been done before at Sun. Some of these included:

- **An analyst treat:** Sun created "**Inside Sun Software Days**"—new analyst events designed to nurture one-on-one relationships with key analysts. These "open kimono" meetings, held semi-annually at Sun's Menlo Park headquarters, gave analysts a wider, deeper look at Sun's R&D and operating priorities. Each of these events was designed to specifically highlight the commitment Sun was making to the WebTone strategy.

- **New approach to direct marketing:** Instead of one "catch all" product-focused direct mail project, Sun executed an approach to reach three audiences separately but simultaneously: CIOs, line-of-business managers, and IT staff. Each target audience received a unique version of a common offer and action plan. Since these three audiences were involved in the sales decision, this direct marketing strategy actively created a one-on-one dialog with each, then encouraged the three audience members to put their pieces together to gain the ultimate benefit.

- **Maintaining the drum beat:** Every speech that McNealy and other top execs made referenced the WebTone. For the next 18 months, every director, when interviewed about their business line, also referenced the WebTone strategy and highlighted how their products fit within it.

- **Worldwide multi-faceted customer reference activities:** Key customers were hand-selected to reinforce specific messaging. These customer stories were executed at precise times during the next year in order to keep a running stream of customer momentum.

Sun's WebTone strategy unfolded like rolling thunder. A snapshot of the initial launch plan is shown in Figure 2. The development of the WebTone campaign strategy began on January 2nd. Execution of activities began April 15 and the drum beat continued for nine months. This WebTone launch plan was designed not to tell the WebTone story all at once, but over time.

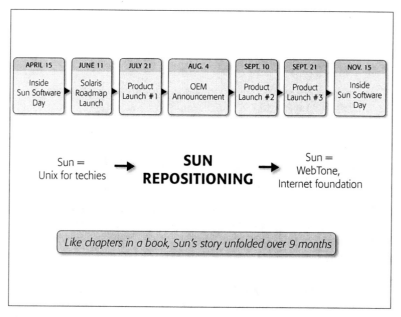

Figure 2: Sun's WebTone Tactical Launch Plan (Phase 1)

Results

McNealy and his team recognized that the stakes were higher. A new approach to marketing was required. Only after the WebTone campaign objective, strategy, and campaign/launch plan (high-level) were approved did the team focus on the execution pieces. Had the marketing team jumped prematurely to execution before developing a thoughtful marketing strategy, these carefully targeted, creative, impactful marketing programs and activities would have been missed.

The WebTone campaign was wildly successful on all accounts. This new approach to campaign development was soon adopted throughout Sun, including its new Java business unit. Some of the results obtained included:

- **14% increase in annual revenue**, driven in part by the WebTone campaign as recognized in the annual report, making Sun a $9.7 billion company by end of fiscal year 1998[4]

- **90 days** to execution! WebTone became the rallying cry.

  - Process initiated January 2

  - 30 days to get to Gate 1 (campaign strategy review with Sun's executive team)

  - 15 days after that to get to Gate 2 (final approval of phase I tactics)

  - Execution plans laid out in detail in time for the first "launch" which took place April 15

- **20-30% faster** execution times (with much less frustration!) for all marketing activities because the strategy and messaging were approved before creative began (i.e., fewer rewrites were required).

- **3X more** press coverage in the following six months than the previous period because the messaging was consistent, focused, and relevant.

- **The 1st of many**: The success of the WebTone campaign led to others, including the "We put the dot in dotcom" campaign.

- **Higher team morale**: The success of the WebTone campaign created a buzz internally. Marketing clearly made a difference, and people took notice.

---

4. Sun Microsystems, Inc. 1998 Annual Report, pages 2, 8, "That's why so much of our efforts this year has been directed toward what we call the WebTone."

Introducing the Integrated Marketing Plan (IMP) template

The centerpiece of the campaign development process is the Integrated Marketing Plan, or IMP. (A template for the IMP is included in the appendix and available online at www.kickstartall.com/campaign_development.html).

Some organizations may prefer to use the term "marketing plan" or "go to market plan." Semantics aside, their purpose is the same as the IMPs. Regardless of which term you prefer, the best practices we will explore in this book equally apply.

There is a lot of confusion about what a good IMP is versus what it is not. In this book, we'll explore what distinguishes a good plan from a dangerous plan, and what marketing leaders need to know. But, before we jump to filling in the blanks, let's take a moment to understand the true value within any IMP. It is not just a document to be filled in.

Building an integrated marketing plan means integrating the ways a company talks to people who buy or don't buy based on what they see, hear, feel, etc. It means planning a dialog to elicit a response, not just conducting a monologue. It means being accountable for results, not just readership scores or counting web hits. And it means delivering a return on investment, not just spending a budget. Planning your integrated marketing communications campaigns is exciting. In today's competitive business world, it's not optional.

So, how do you begin to build an IMP? First off, the IMP is only as good as the collaborative dialog used to create it. By that, I mean that the objectives of a disciplined campaign development process that produces the IMP are:

1. **To guide executive decision-making** surrounding the campaign creation, evolution, and its execution
2. **To drive purposeful, cross-organization, worldwide collaboration** in order to align everyone behind a common set of goals and expectations
3. **To focus worldwide marketing** on the adoption of a consistent campaign development and management process, including terminology and nomenclature

The completed and approved IMP is the final deliverable in the campaign development process. There will be lots of corollary documents created during the development process: messaging matrices, target audience profiles, budget analysis, product definitions, to name only a few. However, the final IMP will become the _executive summary_ summarizing the objectives, strategy, campaign map, and assumptions for each major campaign. It becomes the campaign bible, the central reference that will keep the execution team on strategy. To that end, the IMP helps ensure that all marketing players sing off the same song sheet.

Terminology

One last piece of background we need before we jump into the process is campaign-related terminology. World-class marketers embrace a campaign hierarchy that helps them maintain the focus and clarity of their efforts (see Figure 3).

Figure 3: Understanding the Campaign Hierarchy of Campaigns, Programs, Activities, and Offers

As such, the campaign development process showcased in this book defines the components of the campaign as follows:

Campaign: The combination of marketing programs that support an overarching campaign objective. If we were to use a military analogy, the campaign would indicate the "hill we are going to take." It doesn't tell how the hill will be taken, but it does specify direction and an umbrella business objective. Campaigns may be driven around customer business needs, solution sets, competitive threats, or company/product repositioning.

Example: *The Sun WebTone campaign was a "thought leadership" campaign designed to reposition the company.*

Programs: A collection of marketing activities and offers that are grouped together to achieve a specific marketing objective. Program types include awareness, competitive replacement, cross-sell/up-sell, migration, new customer acquisition, nurturing, and renewal.

Example: *A cross-sell/up-sell program designed to promote a new product bundle.*

Activities: The specific marketing vehicles that deliver an offer.

Example: *A webcast that discusses CIO business problems and solution alternatives.*

Offer: The specific call-to-action that supports a program and its objectives. This is the deliverable that the target audience will receive.

Example: *A solution-focused whitepaper the prospect receives as a result of attending the aforementioned webinar.*

Campaigns versus activities

The number of campaigns your marketing team will be working on depends on your business. But keep in mind that campaigns are not intended to be solely product based; not every product requires its own campaign. Conversely, a good, well-structured campaign may include many products.

Most teams I've worked with started out trying to juggle as many as 10 campaigns, but quickly reduced that number to five or fewer, combining campaigns or eliminating them due to redundancy or because they ended up being of secondary importance. Campaigns are complex, multi-faceted engagement models. Because of this, a campaign must have a clear and direct linkage to the programs, activities and offers that support the achievement of the campaign's objectives. Because of this complexity, I've always found that it is better to have fewer campaigns than many. This drives focus. And focus leads to crisper messages aimed at targeted market segments, tighter differentiation, and higher valued interaction with customers and prospects.

All campaigns will have marketing activities associated with them. However, not all marketing activities will be tied to a campaign. How can this be? This is okay and even expected. Standard business basics like company newsletters, the annual report, customary customer support materials and tools are accepted business practices and need not be force-fit into a campaign structure. We don't need to waste our time forcing all activities into the campaign model. If you have routine marketing tactics that are working well, then we don't need to reinvent them within the campaign process. We want to save our campaign energy for the critical marketing initiatives that will make the most difference to your prospects, customers, and to your sales team.

On your mark. Get set. Go!

This book is about applying the practical lessons learned by Sun and best practices adopted by hi-tech companies such as Aspect, Genesys, Hewlett-Packard, Informatica, and Symantec, and scores of others. Every company is different. But, I guarantee you that 80% of the process steps, templates, and techniques included in this book can be applied to your business with great success. For the other 20%, some customization will be required. This book will help you assess your own needs so you can begin putting these best practices to use, starting today.

2 Secrets of a Best-in-Class Campaign Development Process

The campaign development process is designed to drive, encourage, and optimize collaboration and teamwork across the organization. This chapter describes the basic process being used today by a number of leading high technology companies. Process flow charts, best practices, and practical tips and tricks are shared at each step in the process.

"If you do your homework properly in the development of the communication strategy, it will result in a sharper, more persuasive integrated selling message directed to the most likely prospect." [5]

Don E. Schultz, Professor of Advertising and Integrated Marketing Communications, Northwestern University

5. Don E. Schultz, Stanley I. Tannenbaum, Robert F. Lauterborn, Integrated Marketing Communications, page 65-66, NTB Business Books, 1993

What is the campaign development process, and what triggers it?

Whether your company is executing marketing activities according to a pre-defined plan or via an ad-hoc sixth sense, you are following a campaign development process. A "campaign development process" includes the steps you and your team go through to decide what marketing activity to do when and for which audience. Every company has a process, but they may not recognize it as such. What's more, higher ROI gains are achieved when using processes that are thoughtfully constructed versus those that aren't.

*"But do I need to follow this process for **every** marketing campaign?"* I hear you ask. The campaign development process we're talking about is best used for only the most strategic, complex, high-stakes initiatives. By that I mean entry into a new market or aggressively stealing market share from a competitor. For campaigns that are "business as usual," this process is overkill. Campaigns related to business basics, such as introducing a new set of features or new support options do not require as rigorous a process as described here.

After 20 years of in-the-trenches experience with a number of hi-tech companies as an employee and a consultant, I have discovered several secrets about what type of campaign development process produces consistently better results. Better quality leads, higher awareness levels, improved customer loyalty, and the highest marketing ROI are almost always achieved when marketing functional and regional experts and leaders participate in a structured campaign development process before jumping to the execution. To use another military analogy, this planning process follows the "ready, aim, fire" approach whereby military leaders decide what hill to take and plan how they will take it, prior to deploying the ground forces. The alternative is the "ready, fire, aim" approach which leads to frustration and wasted resources when campaigns have to be redesigned when the hills are re-prioritized but the ground troops have already been deployed.

> *The most important benefit in embracing a campaign development process is that it invites cross-functional participation.*

By its nature, cross-functional participation avoids the problems associated with dictating marketing tactics to the team that they may not understand or agree with based on their own experiences. In the end, when there is a lack of participation in building a balanced campaign strategy, the resulting tactics appear random and unconnected. They fail to produce results or worse, confuse the market.

This chapter is broken down into three parts: an overview of the process, a summary of key roles and responsibilities amongst team members, and answers to some common questions. Here, we'll lay out the basic steps that form the best, most collaborative campaign development process.

Part 1: Overview of the campaign development process

From campaign kickoff to final sign-off

A company's business planning cycle is ongoing (see Figure 4). It begins with the strategic foundation (box #1) which specifies the business goals that must be met, and when they must be met. But, it doesn't prescribe how. The "how" will be developed in the campaign development planning phase (box #2), which is the focus of this book. Once the campaign plan (or integrated marketing plan) has been established, the company moves into the execution phase (box #3). All the while, careful attention is being paid to the reporting of results and fine tuning of the programs (box #4). The final analysis then becomes an input into the next business planning cycle.

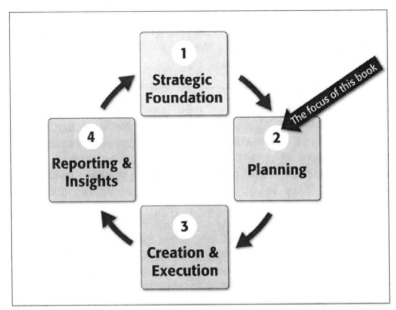

Figure 4: A Company's Business Planning Cycle

We will assume that a company's strategic foundation has already been established and well communicated to the marketing and sales teams. This is an important expectation because campaigns that are not well-grounded end up wasting resources, creating internal frustration, and confusing the target market.

How the most successful companies develop their best campaign plans

First off, I should explain that the campaign development process is not an isolated process. In fact, it is an overlay to the annual business planning, department planning, and budgeting processes that exist in almost every company, large or small. All senior marketing executives ask their directors and department heads to submit a functional plan once a year. This functional plan includes a summary of programs or tactics they plan on executing, along with headcount and budget requirements. Like pieces of a jigsaw puzzle, the marketing managers will produce their piece of the puzzle. Unfortunately, it is not always clear what the puzzle will look like when the pieces are put together. This is where the campaign development process comes into play. When a campaign development process is initiated, it forces the marketing functions to integrate their efforts to a much greater degree. The result is the formation of marketing functional plans that fit together cleanly to produce a crisp, clear picture.

The campaign development process is about **integration, team work, and cross-functional partnership.** In fact, the process is not worked for process' sake; it's worked to encourage the best, most insightful, most collaborative discussions so optimal marketing mix decisions are always reached (see Figure 5). This collaboration results in a 360-degree view of the marketing challenge and opportunity. Through the magic of working the process, all of the marketing media managers (e.g., press relations manager, advertising manager) come together to reinforce and drive an ongoing, meaningful dialog with a prospect or customer that will grow over time and result in a higher degree of customer loyalty.

Why is a formal campaign development process important?

1. It drives purposeful, cross-organization, worldwide collaboration and teamwork.

2. It establishes a consistent, systematic approach for synchronizing multiple (and possibly competing) campaigns.

3. It speeds time-to-production and lowers the development costs of all marketing materials because costly rewrites are avoided.

Figure 5: Campaign Development Process

When a consistent, systematic process is not followed, team members remain siloed. They spend a lot of time debating priorities, strategies, and time tables. Frustration levels rise because decisions are second-guessed. And, the creation of marketing deliverables from press releases to website and collateral design take multiple iterations that would have been unneeded if a stable strategy and direction had been agreed to and communicated widely before production began.

Breaking down the basic campaign development process

Although each company will have a slightly different campaign development process, there are three primary stages that all processes have in common: Kickoff, Synchronization, and Decision (see Figure 6).

Kickoff meetings literally mark the beginning of the collaborative campaign development process. Synchronization meetings are tools used to help the team develop the IMP and address gaps, issues, and road blocks. Because resources are limited and business priorities must be established, a campaign management steering committee is required to provide the proper guidance. This steering committee is designed and run similarly to the product development steering committee. It is an executive body responsible for approving integrated marketing plans for the most strategic campaigns. It is also a point of escalation for resource and budget issues.

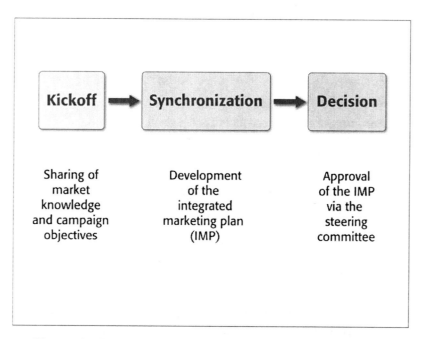

Figure 6: Three Phases of the Campaign Development Process

Marketing campaigns don't build themselves. And, they are not built by a single person. However, they are driven by an anointed campaign manager who has the responsibility and authority for bringing people together to tackle the marketing opportunity. It is critical to understand that while led by a campaign manager, the campaign strategy and tactical plan will be developed by a team via this collaborative process. The designated campaign manager may reside in product marketing, corporate marketing or field marketing. The role of the campaign manager is further explored in Chapter 7.

The Kickoff Meeting: prelude to planning

> **Purpose:** *To educate, inform, and align the marketing team*
>
> **Meeting host:** Campaign manager
>
> **Participants:** A representative from each corporate marketing discipline, product marketing, field or regional marketing and sales
>
> **Agenda:** To introduce the campaign and walk through the primary data and background that is required in order for the functions/regions to develop specific programs to support the campaign.
>
> **Meeting design:** Lecture and Q&A
>
> **Meeting length:** 1-2 hours

The campaign development process officially starts with a public kickoff meeting led by the designated campaign manager. However, before the kickoff meeting is held, some careful preparation is required. In most cases, the CMO or VP of marketing will have named and introduced the marketing campaign concept (sometimes referred to as initiatives) for the fiscal year and then anointed a campaign manager to lead each campaign.

The campaign manager's first duty is to research the opportunity, gather key market and competitive information, and then work with the executive team to confirm the specific goals, objectives, general resource requirements (including rough budget guidelines), and timing of the campaign. This information becomes the solid foundation upon which the campaign details will be built. To be sure, the campaign manager does not do this in isolation. The best campaign managers are politically-savvy marketing leaders; they will interview stakeholders and experts inside and outside the company in order to scope the campaign appropriately. With this information in hand, the campaign manager is ready to introduce the full campaign scope to the rest of the global marketing team. This takes place during the kickoff meeting.

It is important to understand that the kickoff meeting is not about dictating or even brainstorming the marketing tactics (That happens later.) Instead, the kickoff meeting is a prelude to planning. The campaign manager uses this meeting to educate, inform, and direct a larger team of marketing experts who will be called upon to execute the campaign. The campaign manager will also describe the process they will follow during the coming weeks. (See Chapters 4 and 5 for more detail.)

One of the best examples of a kickoff meeting was at Sun where the campaign manager hosted a structured meeting in a style similar to a press briefing. His agenda was clear and concise; he included guest speakers from product marketing to describe the target audience, and a speaker from analyst relations to update the team on a recent analyst report relevant to the industry. There was also plenty of time for questions and answers. During this meeting, he distributed a color-coded, bound set of reference materials that gave further details on the campaign objectives, target audience segmentation, product value proposition, customer references, relevant benchmark statistics, testimonials, and evidence to support their claims of product performance. In short, by the time the meeting concluded, all representatives of his extended team had 80% of the information they would need in order to draft a recommendation for how their function could support the overall campaign. The final 20% would be worked out as team members collaborated in the following weeks. An example of a typical agenda for a kickoff meeting is shown in Figure 7.

The best time to hold a kickoff meeting

Kickoff meetings are usually either tied to the annual planning process or to a specific product launch plan. A typical campaign development process can take between eight and 12 weeks, depending on the complexity of the campaign. Ideally, from a timing standpoint, a typical kickoff meeting is held four to six months prior to the launch/execution date. This allows plenty of time for the team to work the details of the activities and offers once the strategy has been set. (As you will recall with the WebTone example in Chapter 2, the planning-to-first-execution timeline was 90 days: the kickoff meeting was held on January 2, with the first tactical launch executed on April 15.)

Integrated Marketing Plan – Kickoff Meeting Agenda

Welcome and description of the marketing campaign (15 minutes)

- Introduction of the campaign name including a short description
- High-level marketing goals (upon which the success of the campaign will be judged)
- Time table indicating the duration of the campaign and the targeted launch date

Setting the stage (60 minutes)

- Market backgrounder
  - Target market segmentation, including the business problem the target audiences are trying to solve
  - Current (or near future) competitive alternatives
  - Partner or channel implications
  - Q&A
- Relevant product information
  - Product value proposition (as relevant to the intended target audience)
  - Product launch plan (if this is for a new product introduction)
  - Product roadmap (if multiple releases are going to be introduced during the campaign's time frame)
  - Q&A

Next steps (15 minutes)

- Action items for team members
- Where to get additional information
- Campaign development timeline
- Q&A

Figure 7: A Typical Agenda for a Kickoff Meeting

In reality, the team may not have the luxury of this much time. In that case, it is best to host a kickoff meeting as soon as possible after the executive direction has been communicated. But, keep in mind that a well-run kickoff meeting is not just thrown together. It is important that the campaign manager be well prepared to share this information in a coordinated, confident manner. Because businesses are moving quickly, the market analysis may not yet be complete in time for the kickoff meeting. However, there must be a reasonable amount of confidence in the available data and executive sponsorship in order for the campaign to be kicked off.

Who attends the kickoff meeting?

In general, the kickoff meeting is open to anyone who has a need or an interest in the campaign. Since the objective is to educate, inform, and guide, the more widely this information is shared, the better.

Required attendees usually include:

- Product marketing representative(s)

- Partner and channel marketing representative(s)

- Corporate marketing functional representatives from

    - Advertising

    - Press relations

    - Analyst relations

    - Direct marketing

    - Event marketing

    - Collateral

    - Web marketing

- Regional marketing representatives

    - Americas

    - Europe, Middle East, Africa (EMEA)

    - Asia Pacific

    - Japan

- Sales representative or sponsor

Optional attendees may include executives, managers, and individual contributors throughout the organization including customer support, inside sales, and product management.

Tips & Tricks for avoiding the three most common kickoff meeting disasters:

1. **Failing to hold a kickoff meeting:** When campaign managers decide they don't need one, they fail to engage the team that will be responsible for executing the marketing tactics. As such, the individuals never develop a common frame of reference, nor do they feel that they are part a larger team with a common goal. This lack-of-connection encourages siloed behavior and the development of discrete marketing tactics that are not integrated. It also encourages regions to (continue to) act independently from headquarters.

2. **Dictating the details of the marketing plan:** Sometimes campaign managers go too far and prescribe specific marketing tactics at this meeting. The meeting and their role then become political because this approach implies the campaign manager has direct authority over the team, which is not usually true. Thus, it causes all kinds of frustration and angst within the team.

   A good campaign manager will likely have some rich insight and knowledge about the market, region, or the marketing activities which will apply best. But, an experienced campaign manager will know that campaigns for large, multinational companies are complex by nature and must have cross-functional cooperation in order to develop and then execute a balanced campaign. He or she will invite the appropriate individuals to participate in the planning process, thereby gaining their wisdom, knowledge, and most importantly their commitment to execute the plan with their full energy and a positive attitude.

3. **Failure to describe the process:** Whether or not this is the first time the team has gone through the campaign development process, the campaign manager must always end their meeting with a clear roadmap of next steps so the team members know what is expected of them. Milestones, due dates, and timetables must be clearly communicated. If team members leave the meeting unclear on what they need to do next, the meeting has failed.

Synchronization Meetings: building the IMP

Purpose: *To develop a working draft of the Integrated Marketing Plan*

Meeting facilitator: Campaign manager

Participants: A representative from each corporate marketing discipline, product marketing, field or regional marketing and sales.

Agenda: For the marketing media experts to share program recommendations, identify gaps, and gather feedback on where/how their function can support the achievement of the campaign objective.

Meeting design: Collaborative working sessions conducted over several weeks.

Meeting length: 4 – 8 hours each, depending on the agenda

What are synchronization meetings?

Having conducted the kickoff meeting, the team is now grounded in a common understanding of the marketing opportunity and the campaign-level goals. With that as background, the focus of the next eight–twelve weeks will be on developing an IMP.

A synchronization meeting is a structured brainstorming, collaborative session where the team comes together to get real work done in constructing the IMP. An IMP template is provided so team members can collect their thoughts and share recommendations (e.g., functional goals, objectives, metrics, programs and activities). As each member presents their material, the others ask questions, helping to identify gaps and overlaps and ultimately construct a comprehensive campaign.

Throughout this process, there will be a series of synchronization meetings, some formal, some informal. Whereas formal synchronization meetings are structured as ½ day or day-long practical working sessions, informal synchronizations may take place daily between individuals. There is no question that some of the most insightful recommendations and creative ideas will be generated in these collaborative sessions. Depending on the complexity of the campaign, more or fewer of these synchronization meetings will be required.

Each formal synchronization meeting will be moderated by the campaign manager. Participants include functional and regional representatives. The objectives of the synchronization meeting series include:

To develop the first or subsequent draft of the IMP

- To hear functional/regional recommendations and build a comprehensive view of the total campaign and the supporting programs (at a high level)

- To look for gaps, potential synergies with other campaigns, as well as risks and dependencies

- To discuss and debate implications and areas for further refinement

- To get a rough idea of resource and budget requirements

Four types of synchronization meetings

Depending on the complexity of the campaign or the extent of the global reach of the campaign, multiple synchronization meetings may be required. There are four types of synchronization meetings; some of these may be combined.

> *By synchronizing the media, you are deploying a cohesive sustained dialog rather than the fragmented scattershot of messages often experienced by customers or prospects.*

Synchronization Meeting #1: Architecting the campaign map

This is the first synchronization meeting and usually takes place one week after the kickoff meeting. The focus of this meeting is on the strategy and programs (not the tactics) that support the campaign. The goal is to produce a campaign map – literally a mapping of the set of agreed-upon programs that will comprise the overall campaign. (Recall the WebTone campaign map shown in Figure 1.) Chapter 4 explores the concept and purpose of the campaign map. The goal of synchronization meeting #1 is to rally the team in support of which, and how many, of these programs are necessary to achieve the campaign's objective.

Synchronization Meeting #2: Aligning multiple campaigns

Synchronization meeting #2 is a reality check. When companies are running multiple campaigns, it makes sense to synchronize the campaigns to understand where they overlap. Overlaps can commonly occur with common target audiences, products, vehicles, and timeframes. For example, one company was running five campaigns thought to be unique. However, as the campaign maps for each were developed, they discovered that three of the campaigns were targeting the same audiences (CIOs of Fortune 500 companies) at the same time (April) with some of the same products. By discovering this overlap, they decided to combine two of the three campaigns, and to shift the third campaign for execution later in the year.

With the campaign map now illustrated, an executive summary of the campaign strategy is produced and then shared with the steering committee at the Gate 1 review meeting. Once approved, the team is ready to prescribe the supporting activities and offers that will make up each supporting program. Those will be generated during the synchronization #3 meeting.

Synchronization Meeting #3: Developing program blueprints

Synchronization meeting #3 is about diving into the specific activities and offers that make up each of the recommended programs. As such, each program will have a blueprint that shows how the combination of media types is used to create a personalized, engaging dialog with the intended audience. Chapter 5 introduces the blueprint concept and details the seven basic program blueprint types. The campaign team will work from these models to determine which ones apply and then customize them to meet their specific market needs.

It is important to understand that we are still in the planning stage – not the execution stage. This means that we want to map out a path for engaging a specific target audience so as to communicate a specific message or message theme. This is not about tactical planning where we list out every action item for every email that will be deployed during the course of the program. Those tactics will be captured, managed, and monitored during the execution phase of the campaign; but that level of detail is not appropriate during the planning process.

Synchronization Meeting #4: Aligning regional activities

Synchronization meeting #4 is also a reality check. When multiple campaigns are intended to be introduced within a region at the same time, the execution of those activities may be constrained by the limited regional resources. To help avoid miss-set expectations and disappointment, a separate synchronization meeting may be needed for regional managers to prioritize the multiple campaigns and their supporting programs. Conducting this synchronization meeting early can help teams avoid producing blueprints that will never be acted upon in the regions.

Three secrets for managing successful synchronization meetings

Synchronization meetings can be wildly successful or downright painful. What makes the difference? The secrets to success are the following:

1. **Structured meetings:** The campaign manager provides structure to the work session. This means that the campaign manager will act as a moderator and will develop a crisp agenda with a clearly-stated meeting objective. The campaign manager ensures that all participants have a chance to contribute and be heard. They are also in charge of taking notes and capturing action items.

2. **Active participation:** Team members are active participants in the meeting, assisting the campaign manager at each stage of the campaign development process. All participants come prepared to share their insights and recommendations, having completed any assigned pre-work.

3. **Professional engagement:** Only constructive dialog is allowed. Ground rules are set and reinforced to encourage open and honest discussion that is respectful of all team members.

Decision: steering committee review meetings

Purpose: *To gain approval of the IMP at Gate 1 and Gate 2*

Meeting host: Chairman of the steering committee, usually the VP of marketing operations

Participants: Steering committee members

Guests: The campaign manager and selected team members who will participate in the presentation

Meeting design: Presentation and Q&A

Meeting length: Typically 60 minutes per team presentation

For large multinational companies, marketing campaigns can be complex and detailed. This is especially tricky when multiple campaigns may be initiated at the same time with overlapping objectives. When resources are limited, business priorities must be established. A campaign management steering committee is required to provide the proper guidance. As mentioned earlier, the steering committee is an executive body responsible for approving integrated marketing plans for the most strategic campaigns. It is also a point of escalation for resource and budget issues.

The steering committee review is not to be taken lightly. The campaign team must be fully prepared to present their campaign strategy for Gate 1 review and then the program details for Gate 2 review. They must have their facts straight and be prepared to describe and even defend their recommendations.

Campaign management steering committee, defined:

- Comprised of VPs of marketing operations, product marketing, marketing communications, field marketing, regional marketing

- Focuses on strategic topics related to marketing messaging, communications, and customer engagement models and methodologies

- Makes operational decisions regarding campaign development, prioritization, regional considerations, and resource allocations (budget and headcount)

- Reviews and approves (or disapproves) the IMP at two phases:

  - Gate 1: approval of the campaign strategy, including the campaign map

  - Gate 2: approval of the program blueprints that include the recommended activities and offers

Why are there two steering committee reviews?

The objective of the Gate 1 review is to set forth the campaign strategy, including the resource requirements, necessary for success before work actually begins on the tactics. Countless hours and dollars have been lost in marketing activities being developed that later got cancelled or flat out missed their mark. Gate 1 is intended to help guide and reinforce team decisions so these precious resources are not wasted. (See Figure 8 for an example of a typical Gate 1 agenda.) Only once Gate 1 has been reached and approved, will the teams be allowed to focus on the specific activities and offers that will comprise the overall campaign.

Integrated Marketing Plan – Campaign Strategy Review
Agenda – Gate 1

- Campaign name & description
- Campaign objective(s)
- Value proposition
- Campaign map
- Tactical calendar (program view only)
- Rough budget estimate
- Key assumptions
- Synergies with other campaigns
- Open issues requiring steering committee guidance

Figure 8: A Typical Agenda for a Gate 1 Review Meeting

The objective of the Gate 2 review is to roll up all of the program blueprints (and their activities and offers) to evaluate how they all fit together. A sample of a Gate 2 agenda is shown in Figure 9.

Integrated Marketing Plan – Program Blueprints Review
Agenda Gate 2

- Summary of revisions from Gate 1 meeting
- Overview of key program blueprints
- Program Executive Summaries
    - Program name, description, and objectives
    - Program blueprints (showing the connections between activities and offers)
    - Program calendar of major events
- Synergies with other campaigns and/or programs
- Open issues requiring steering committee guidance

Figure 9: A Typical Agenda for a Gate 2 Review Meeting

During this review session, campaign teams can and should highlight gaps and overlaps and risks associated with being able to successfully deploy the campaign. Occasionally, campaigns will overlap and teams will be fighting for limited resources. In this forum, the steering committee can address those issues, make real-time decisions, and provide final guidance to the team as they prepare to execute the tactics of the campaign.

In addition to these two formal meetings, the steering committee is a resource to help resolve escalations. When issues arise due to changing market dynamics, product road maps, launch plans, etc, the campaign manager may decide to engage the steering committee to get guidance and resolve issues earlier rather than later.

Putting it all together

Figure 10 shows the general process steps from the kickoff meeting to the final steering committee review meeting.

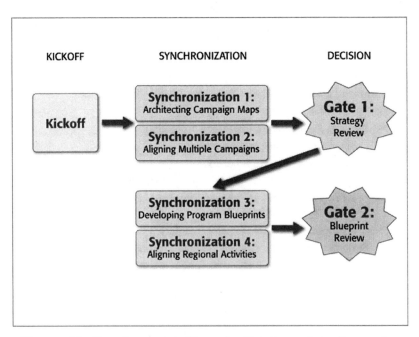

Figure 10: Fundamental Steps in the Complete Campaign Development Process

Despite these formal steps, much work gets accomplished during informal and impromptu meetings which I term "mini-syncs." These hallway conversations and small group sessions can be incredibly productive. I've observed that cultures that encourage delegation and personal initiative produce the best plans quickly. It is important to note that every company will have nuances about this process that will be unique for their organization. However, the basic process steps will be very similar.

Part 2: Roles and responsibilities

I am commonly asked to describe the roles and responsibilities of players involved in this process. Although each company has its own uniqueness, Figure 11 provides some typical definitions and descriptions that will help you set some team, and individual expectations.

Department	Responsibilities
Campaign Management	Responsible for team coordination and managing the development of the IMP. Owner of the IMP process and author of the final IMP document.
Corporate Marketing	Responsible for designing and executing the marketing media strategies and tactics (e.g. press releases, global lead generation programs, webinars, website, events, advertising).
Field Marketing	Responsible for lead qualification and development of viable sales opportunities; supplements corporate marketing plan with local activities & offers (with an effort to leverage corporate marketing resources & materials).
Marketing Executive	Responsible for sponsoring the overall campaign; ensures alignment with company goals; removes roadblocks.
Partner Marketing	Responsible for representing partner needs in the campaign development process; acts as the interface and liaison between corporate marketing and the partners.
Product Marketing (outbound-focused)	Responsible for product strategy, target market segmentation, messaging, and content creation.
Sales Representative	Represents sales priorities and objectives; provides input into the campaign development process; also communicates campaign status to the rest of the sales team.
Steering Committee	Responsible for approving and prioritizing the campaign plans and resolving escalated issues that impact the successful execution of the campaign.

Figure 11: Basic Roles and Responsibilities

Part 3: Answers to the four most common questions about the process

Who is responsible for the campaign development process?

In most cases, a technology company will have a VP or senior director of marketing operations responsible for constructing the umbrella campaign development process. This person (or team) will also be responsible for producing the tools and templates, as well as training the rest of the organization in how to engage the process. The campaign managers may or may not report to the operations staff. Regardless, they will be working together closely to adopt and adapt the process in real time.

When do you need a campaign manager?

Not all companies may need a formal campaign manager role. Smaller businesses that sell only a few products to a few audiences may indeed be able to manage the complexities of their campaigns within the structure of their current marketing team. However, if yours is a company with annual revenue of more than $50M, markets in more than one geographic region, and a marketing budget of any amount, you can benefit greatly by making use of a campaign manager. Other factors include your specific campaign or product launch objectives, the breadth of your product offerings, or the number of targeted market segments you want to actively pursue. The more strategic or critical your marketing objectives, the more value a campaign manager can bring.

There is always a cost inflicted by a lack of strategic forethought and coordination. Although that cost may be intangible to upper management, it is nevertheless very real. Once a company reaches this size and complexity, it is guaranteed that some marketing dollars will be wasted and opportunities will be missed without the guidance and marketing discipline a professional campaign manager can bring.

Is the IMP meant to be a tactical marketing plan?

No. Remember, the IMP is not a tactical marketing plan. It is not intended to be the Gantt chart of all tactics and all action items. There are other tools better used for that once you pass Gate 2 and then get into the execution phase (which is outside the scope of the IMP). Instead, the IMP links activities and offers to programs and campaigns. Chapter 5 describes the level of detail appropriate in planning blueprints. For now, don't get caught in the weeds.

How often do these campaigns get updated?

After an IMP has been approved at Gate 2, you're now in execution mode. It's tempting to think that planning is now complete. But it's not. The world continues to evolve and your business conditions will change too. Therefore, it is best to review the IMP once each quarter, and plan a formal review with the steering committee every six months. That way, you have the ability to make changes proactively. The campaign manager's job is to keep an eye on the campaign and how the market is responding to it. He or she will track campaign results and report back to the steering committee during quarterly or semi-annual checkpoint meetings.

3 Setting the Foundation of Your Campaign

Every successful marketing campaign rests on three solid pillars that will define its strategy: a focused and concise campaign description, a clearly-stated, appropriate campaign objective, and a well-constructed value proposition. Chapter 3 discusses each pillar, offering tips and tricks to create each and evaluate them for best performance.

"Vision without action is a daydream. Action without vision is a nightmare." [6]
Japanese proverb

The three pillars that define a marketing campaign's success

This chapter is about setting clear campaign objectives, defining the campaign, and constructing a crisp value proposition before deciding upon which marketing activities to execute. Because of today's fast pace of business, many marketers

---

6. http://quotes.prolix.nu/Authors/?Japanese_proverb

fall into the trap of rushing to execution without first taking the initial steps to plan the campaign. As a result, they produce "marketing popcorn" – activities that are discrete and unconnected. Although each activity may be highly creative, if they don't engage the prospect in a dialog or help move them along their buying process, the activities are largely a waste of time and money.

Pillar 1: Defining the marketing campaign

The campaign name and description is a very simple concept, yet it is so simple that it is often overlooked and assumed. Not having a documented description leads to misconceptions about what it is and what it is not. An example of a campaign name and description is shown in Figure 12.

Campaign Name: Securing the Desktop

Campaign Description: For this fiscal year, our "securing the desktop" story will continue and expand across all segments within the manufacturing and services industries, not just the small business/home office sector where we have already gained traction. Expansion will reach into prioritized industry segments of the upper mid-market and lower enterprise market and include a new services bundling of core products with our advanced server products. This campaign will kickoff in Q2 and run for 18 months.

Figure 12: Example of a Campaign Name and Description

Campaign name: A few words that communicate a theme or focus for the campaign.

Campaign description: A few sentences describing the campaign and its context.

Marketing campaigns, as we have said, represent major initiatives within the company. Usually the CMO or a strategic marketing team will determine the name and description of the campaign. As significant energy, personnel, time, and investment will be made available to support them, there are usually fewer than five campaigns running at any given time. This is because campaigns are complex and difficult to manage more than a few at a time. It is imperative that everyone is clear on the basic campaign concept; otherwise misalignment and frustration are guaranteed.

Pillar 2: Constructing a "campaign-level" marketing objective

In the context of this book, the term "campaign" means the grander scope of the collection of the marketing programs, activities and offers that will be linked together to drive a campaign-level result. Having said that, it is important to understand that each element of the campaign (e.g., each direct mail piece or web promotion) will also have its own supporting, specific objective. All of those objectives need to add up to support the campaign-level objective. One way to think about the campaign-level objective is to project ourselves into the future: *once all the marketing programs, activities, offers have been executed, what do we hope to accomplish or achieve?*

> *The campaign objective drives the programs and marketing activities.*

There is a lot of confusion surrounding what makes a good campaign-level objective. Because broader metrics can be difficult to measure, marketers are occasionally drawn to more tactical metrics. For example, one vice-president of marketing told me that his campaign objective was to build a website and generate traffic. At the other extreme, one CMO told me his campaign objective was to generate $50M in revenue. Both of these examples are wrong for different reasons, which I will get to shortly. Examples of good campaign objectives are shown in Figure 13. Notice what these examples have in common: they are specific, with a number that can be measured, and a timeframe. These are good examples because they set a clear context for a variety of supporting marketing programs and activities.

Examples of good campaign-level marketing objectives

- To grow North American market-share by 15% within 18 months by stealing deals away from competitor X
- To introduce product Y and establish a presence in the European market with a 15% market-share within 2 years
- To lower cost/lead by $25 and improve marketing conversion rates by 20% by Q4 for Product Z

Figure 13: Good Campaign-Level Objectives

Now let's take a look at a couple of poor examples which unfortunately, are quite common. "Generating traffic" is a poor example of a campaign-level metric because it is not directly tied to a business, financial or market-share outcome. The common misperception of "traffic equals sales" has wasted tremendous amounts of business' capital on the creation of poor-quality websites that don't provide relevant information or engage the visitor. In addition, some CEOs have developed negative attitudes towards marketing by concluding that poor marketing ROI was strictly the result of poor execution rather than lack of a clear and proper objective. No amount of brilliant execution can make up for a lackluster, unclear, or erroneous marketing objective.

"Generating $50M" is also a poor example of a campaign-level objective, but for a different reason. This objective is really a business or sales objective, not a marketing objective. Marketers must be crystal clear in identifying metrics and expectations that their actions can control. In this case, marketing owns only the first steps in the sales process: typically awareness to lead qualification. The final steps of generating proposals and closing sales are the responsibility of the sales team. Hence, to state a marketing campaign objective where marketing does not have the authority and responsibility to carry it through to the end is unfair and inappropriate. More on metrics will be covered in Chapter 6.

Focus and direction come as a result of setting clear, specific objectives. The campaign objective is the central purpose for the campaign. It's a rallying cry for the marketing and sales troops to stand behind and align their actions. If objectives are not carefully chosen, the campaign will succeed only because of luck. And luck is not a sustainable marketing strategy. When campaign objectives are not clearly identified, it is likely the campaign will fail and waste money by trying to sell to people who aren't interested in purchasing your goods and services. Thus, the clearer and more focused your campaign objective, the lower your marketing costs, and the greater your marketing ROI.

Six steps to developing strong campaign-level marketing objectives

1. Be specific: What is the "big picture" result you want to achieve via this campaign? Even at the campaign-level, every objective must have a specific result in mind. The easiest way to be specific is to use numbers to quantify your objectives.

2. Must be measurable: All of your marketing objectives need to be measurable. Otherwise how will you know if you reach them? What clue will you have? Include the qualifiers of time and type as well as how many.

3. Must be realistic: Setting goals that require Herculean efforts probably won't be received well. Similarly, setting goals that are easily achievable won't be taken seriously. There is a balance to setting stretch goals that can be reasonably achieved and exceeded. Only you know what is realistic for your business and your team. Consider the resources you have available such as personnel (and their skill sets), time, technology, and money.

4. Have a time schedule: Identify a time horizon for the life of this campaign. Keep in mind that campaigns focus on the big picture, but the big picture may change over time. As such, campaign horizons are most often multi-quarter. When campaigns are envisioned to be multi-year, break them down into phases. This will allow campaign teams an opportunity to re-evaluate the campaign's progress and reset objectives and expectations at appropriate intervals.

5. Must be compatible: The marketing campaign must be designed in such a way that it is compatible with everything else going on in the company. Cross-organization alignment with sales, customer support, product management and other teams is very important. If marketing has a campaign objective to grow market-share in Europe, but sales is focused on North America, there is an obvious problem.

6. Must be documented: The major advantage to writing down your campaign objective is to be able to communicate to others in the organization as well as having a ready reference guide. Only if it is documented and shared will it be "real" and be acted upon with confidence and determination.

Pillar 3: Building a well-constructed value proposition

While many of us will recognize a good well-thought-out value proposition when we see one, working the process takes practice. There is a lot of confusion about what good value propositions are and what they are not. To understand the secrets of what separates an impactful value proposition from a lame one, we first need to understand how the concept of a value proposition has evolved.

In their 2006 *Harvard Business Review* article entitled, "Customer Value Propositions in Business Markets," Jamie Anderson, James Narus, and Wouter van Rossum classify three types of value propositions: All Benefits, Favorable Points of Difference, and Resonating Focus (or Just What the Customer Values).[7] See Figure 14.

Some marketers are tempted to simply list all the benefits they believe that their offering might deliver to target customers. The more they can think of, the better, so they think. The problem: do customers really care about every benefit?

---

7. James C. Anderson, James A. Narus, and Wouter van Rossum, Customer Value Propositions in Business Markets, Harvard Business Review, March 2006.

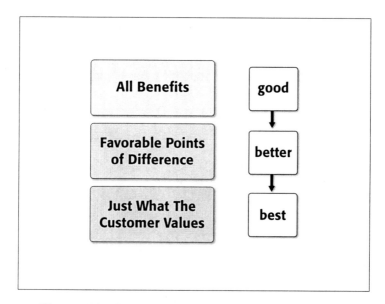

Figure 14: Three Flavors of Value Propositions

Other marketers go further to consider that the customer has an alternative. Unfortunately, they often make the mistake of assuming that any favorable points of difference they can identify and articulate must therefore also be of equal importance to the customer. The problem: saying your solution is better than competitor X's is only relevant if the customer is viewing competitor X's solution as an alternative.

But, best-practice marketers base their value proposition on only those few elements that matter most to target customers, focusing on the clear, differentiated value relevant to that particular target market segment. Then they are able to demonstrate the superiority of their offering and communicate it in a way that conveys a sophisticated understanding of the target segment's business priorities.

Being able to understand "just what the customer values" gives marketers the advantage by showing them how and where to focus the marketing campaign for optimum success.

A best-practice value proposition template

A best-practice value proposition template (as shown in Figure 15 and Appendix A) helps marketers by putting the customer, not their product, in the center of the universe. The key elements are: Customer Set, Problem/Need, Value Driver, Competitive Positioning, and Evidence. Let's take a look at these, one at a time.

Customer Set:			
Problem/Need	**Value Driver**	**Competitive Positioning**	**Evidence**
Summary Statement:			

Figure 15: Value Proposition Template

Customer Set: Successful marketing starts with an exact answer to the question *Who?* The closer the match between your message and the specific type of prospect you want to engage, the more quality leads you will get, and the higher your marketing ROI. "But Mike," I hear you say, "we sell to everyone! Defining our customer set narrowly won't work for us."

By asking *who*, what we're really doing is prioritizing which market segments we will market to proactively. Here's the harsh reality:

1. The average person (you and I) is subjected to more than 10,000 messages everyday! Marketing messages hit us from all sides: from the time you wake up to the news on the radio, read the paper at breakfast, drive by countless billboards, talk with colleagues and friends, surf the Internet, etc. The challenge for us marketers is to figure out how to cut through this noise and clutter. What can we do to make sure our messages get heard and acted upon?

2. Unless you are sitting on top of King Solomon's mines, you don't have enough money or resources to execute campaigns for every possible audience.

The answer to facing these realities is that when it comes to proactive marketing outreach, we need to focus and prioritize our target audiences. This doesn't mean we won't sell our products to folks outside of our target segmentation. We will. We just won't proactively market to them.

You will experience a higher marketing ROI by executing a focused campaign aimed at a specific audience with tailored messages, rather than trying to blanket everyone in every industry at the same time.

Throwing your message out to *everybody* and hoping the right people will find it is like dropping 100,000 copies of a letter addressed to your Aunt Marge in Phoenix out of an airplane as you fly over Arizona. Maybe she'll get it; maybe she won't. It would have been a lot more cost-effective to address your message to a very specific address —Aunt Marge's—and forward it directly to her. Likewise, if you want to work with *first-time* buyers, your advertising and marketing efforts will be much more effective and cost-efficient if you gear the message specifically to them and place your messages *specifically where they will see it.*

So, in choosing a specific target audience, let me define Customer Set as follows:

A Customer Set = an actual group of customers for a given type of offering who have a common set of needs and who reference each other.

A customer set is made up of real people who can be found for marketing purposes. They are factual, not fictional. Different customers can indeed be grouped together if they reference each other. If CIOs in manufacturing reference CIO colleagues in telecommunications companies, then they can be combined into a singular customer set. However, if hotel managers don't reference auto mechanics, then they are best thought of as two distinct customer sets that need to be marketed to separately.

Problem/Need: Many marketers get caught up in thinking about their product or service in isolation of the customers' world. Marketers will push a specific feature or feature set (i.e., it's fast, small, and has more storage space). But what problems do those features help solve? What is the customer's business problem that needs to be addressed? Simply stated, the "problem/need" can be defined as:

Problem/Need = a description of the business or operational problem the target audience needs to address or solve.

The Problem/Need is only the first step in understanding what makes our customers and prospects tick. Marketers can be better served when they think about the customers "value driver" where the value driver is defined as follows:

A Value Driver = a business, financial, operational, technological, or personal outcome and a metric that a specific customer set can use to determine the value of your offering.

It is imperative that we be able to map specific outcomes and metrics that are relevant to a specific target audience. For example, if we know that the CEOs in our target segment are highly concerned about increasing their return on assets, they are probably interested in measuring improvements related to revenues and profit, or reducing business risk. Therefore, we need to identify a specific problem/need that our product or solution can address.

Figure 16 maps likely outcomes and metrics for specific target audiences. These are the elements of their value drivers. It's up to us marketers to figure out which ones best map to specific audiences.

	Outcomes	Metrics
CxO	Higher return on assets	Higher revenue or profit; reduced risk; increased stock price
Line of Business Manager	Operational improvements	Lower customer acquisition costs; improved customer satisfaction
IT Manager	Lower total cost of ownership	Lower price; reduced support costs; faster time to deployment
Technologist	Great features and benefits	Faster processor; less coding required

Figure 16: Value Driver Elements Including Outcomes and Their Metrics

Competitive positioning: In building our value proposition, we must be aware of competitive alternatives. There is always competition, even for brand-new, never-seen-before products. This is because customers always have options, even if the option is to do nothing. Therefore, marketers need to consider each major competitive alternative and position their product or service against it.

Competitive Positioning = **establishing a differentiated value to a customer set by comparing your offering to that of your nearest competitor.**

In conducting a side-by-side analysis of our product or service to that of Competitor X, we may find many differences. But, this is not enough. We need to zero in on the most relevant and meaningful difference as it relates to the customer's expectation and experience. In other words, when we compare our solution to that of Competitive X, what is our strongest differentiator that the customer will care about? Since time and money are limited, we would be wise to streamline our efforts to constantly promote that difference, rather than trying to blanket a variety of differences, some of which may not be relevant.

The bubble-chart shown in Figure 17 is an example of a way to summarize the competitive themes as they relate to different competitors. For IT managers seeking energy-efficient servers, this example contrasts three competitors and the best differentiator against each. The competitor is on the left, your product or service is in the center, and the strongest point of differentiation is on the right. Obviously, some meaningful analysis is behind this simple graphic, but the story that it tells is clear and focused. A decision to focus on a specific competitive positioning and to align key messages behind it will be critically important for breaking through the noise and clutter in the marketplace.

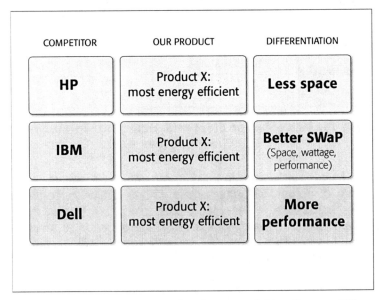

Figure 17: A Technique for Summarizing Competitive Differentiators

Evidence: The final, and perhaps most critical, piece of the value proposition is evidence. What makes you credible in the eyes of your customers and prospects? How can you substantiate the claims you make and the position you so desperately want?

Evidence = **undisputable facts that establish credibility by offering substantiation that your message is accurate and true.**

Evidence may take the form of customer testimonials, benchmark studies, analyst's reviews, third-party product comparisons and analysis. However, in our rush to market, we sometimes take shortcuts that result in common evidence mistakes such as those listed in Figure 18.

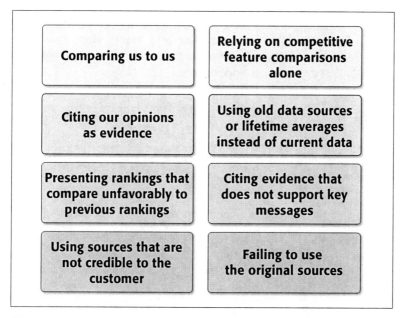

Figure 18: Common Evidence Mistakes That Can Cripple a Campaign

The best place to start in our search for evidence is not "What evidence is available?" Instead, we should ask, "What evidence is needed to make the strongest, most credible value proposition?" To that end, we may need to do some homework to collect the required evidence. Once we decide on what proof points we need, we can develop an action plan to generate it. Let me be clear: we are not talking about manufacturing evidence. We are talking about taking action in order to collect the evidence we need. Actions may include: interviewing customers to understand what ROI and metrics they have achieved using our products or services; arranging for third party product comparisons; talking with analysts; conducting updated benchmark studies. What's at stake here is nothing short of a company's ethics and moral standing. Customers and prospects can tell the difference and will act accordingly.

Putting it all together: We've carefully analyzed the market and prioritized our market segmentation. Now, we are ready to put the pieces of the value proposition together in a short statement.

Figure 19 illustrates an example of a value proposition based on a real product. The names of the company and the product have been omitted for confidentiality. Further background information regarding this example is provided in Appendix A.

Customer Set: CIOs who need to quickly ramp datacenter capacity

Problem/Need	Value Driver	Competitive Positioning	Evidence
A rapidly deployable, more flexible, and less costly datacenter	Mobile datacenters that can be deployed anywhere in 1/10th the time	The world's first virtual, modular datacenter housed in a standard shipping container	Demonstrated density, energy savings, customer testimonials, industry analyst reports

Summary Statement: Only Product X lets you build and deploy a complete datacenter anywhere in the world in 1/10th the time of traditional datacenters, while maximizing space, power and cooling, cutting costs and delivering more capacity per square foot.

Figure 19: Example Value Proposition Template Based on a Real Product

The template format is a good way to summarize the upshot. However, there are two audiences we need to include in our final evaluation of our value proposition: internal leaders, and external experts. By failing to socialize our value proposition with internal leaders, we may inadvertently create political trauma. Everyone has an opinion; and some matter more than others. In any case, every opportunity to socialize, review, and further focus the value proposition is time well spent. Having said that, sometimes these meetings with highly opinionated team members can be unhelpful if they aren't structured. One way to guide these discussions is by using an agenda such as the following:

1. Ask the internal leader/expert to summarize the offering in non-technical jargon.
2. What business problem does our offering alleviate?
3. What's really new?
4. So what? Why does this matter?
5. Of the top 10 features and benefits, which ones are "firsts," "bests," and "onlys?"*

---

* Firsts, bests, and onlys:

- Were we first to market? Which features or benefits can we claim to be first in providing?

- What do we do better than the competition? Which features or benefits can we claim to be the best at delivering?

- What is truly unique about our solution? What aspects of our solution can we claim to be the only provider of?

Lastly, companies can be well served by testing their value proposition with external experts. Test the value proposition with friendly customers who will tell you, constructively, what they really think. Look for formal, as well as informal, ways to test the value proposition with focus groups or your Customer Advisory Board, or key partners. And, understand what the media is writing about so you can align your story with media interests.

Conducting a thoughtful value proposition exercise does take some time. Make the investment. With a succinct value proposition in hand, you will be able to:

- become relevant to your target audience,

- construct focused, meaningful messages more easily, and

- dramatically shorten the time needed to create impactful print and web collateral because they will require fewer rewrites with a whole lot less frustration.

Your competitors are making use of value proposition best practices, and so should you.

4 Working the Process: Part 1 – Sketching the Campaign Map

With the process described in Chapter 2, marketing leaders need a template to guide the cross-functional team in developing a creative, integrated marketing plan (IMP) and the accompanying campaign map. Chapter 4 introduces the IMP template and describes how it is used to achieve approval of the campaign strategy at the Gate 1 review meeting.

"Plans are nothing. Planning is everything." [8]
Dwight D. Eisenhower, General and US President

Working the IMP process

Plans in and of themselves are not nearly as important as the exploration and collaboration found in the planning process. It is through this process that a creative *integrated* campaign strategy and plan will emerge. And in turn, this plan will become the compass that will guide the execution of its programs and activities.

8. Brainy Quote, http://tinyurl.com/2jytvv

I prefer the term *integrated marketing plan* precisely because of the key word "integrated." World-class marketing plans are "integrated" along several dimensions: integrated across a media mix, integrated across a product portfolio, integrated in messaging, and integrated appropriately for local, regional, and global deployment. It's a big word filled with opportunities for producing competitive differentiation.

However, we can sometimes get lost in the details surrounding any plan. The line between strategy and tactics can easily become blurred. With that in mind, the IMP is meant to be a guiding tool, not the only tool. Semantics aside, let us define the IMP in the following way:

> **The IMP is the executive summary for a specific marketing campaign.** *Each marketing campaign will have its own IMP. It summarizes the marketing objectives, strategy, campaign map and assumptions. It is designed to be a tool to guide the development of the marketing campaign strategy and a standard format for communicating this strategy to other internal audiences.*

IMPs vary from company to company. However, the best IMPs always contain the same basic information. A template of a best-practice IMP is shown in Appendix B.

The objective of the Integrated Marketing Plan

The value in any template is not the template, per se. It's the thought process and discussion than accompanies the use of the template. In short, a good template will help you bring the right issues to the table at the right time so the best, optimal marketing decisions can always be made. This is especially true for the IMP. As we introduced in Chapter 1, the primary objectives of the IMP are the following:

1. **To guide executive decision-making** surrounding the campaign creation, evolution, and its execution

2. **To drive purposeful, cross-organization, worldwide collaboration** in order to align everyone behind a common set of goals and expectations

3. **To focus worldwide marketing** on the adoption of a consistent campaign development and management process, including terminology and nomenclature

Regardless of whether you are a Fortune 500 leader or an up-and-coming start-up, world-class marketing campaigns start with a documented strategy and plan. To be sure, every company has nuances that are different, thus requiring tailoring to any templates. Yet, the questions that must be addressed are very much the same. These questions range from *Which target market segments should we prioritize and what is the best way to engage them?* to *What is the optimum marketing mix?* To address these questions, a good IMP can be broken down into two parts, each dealing with one of these sets of questions.

Part 1, covered in this chapter, is about documenting the marketing strategy and crafting a high-level campaign map. Part 2, covered in chapter 5, is about designing effective program blueprints that specifically link activities and offers together to guide a meaningful dialog with the intended audience – hence the optimum marketing mix.

What the IMP is not

The IMP is not . . .

- the execution plan
- a positioning and messaging playbook
- a budget analysis
- a market requirements document (MRD)
- a product requirements document (PRD)
- a document to be shared with customers or channel partners

There are a lot of documents created by marketers to help them do their jobs: PR plans, messaging matrices, launch plans, collateral creative briefs, and so on. While those documents and tools are critically important for us in the execution of the tactics of our job, they are not productive for engaging a global marketing team in the formation of a marketing strategy and comprehensive plan. You might think of those documents as the individual pieces of the puzzle. But unless you know what the picture on the box is, you will struggle to figure out how to put the pieces together in the right way.

Alternatively, some people view the planning process as requiring attention to every tiny detail, resulting in a ream of paperwork that few people will ever read.

> **The cold, hard fact is that people don't have the time or energy to read the fine print; people want a clear and crisp summary that logically lays out the marketing game plan. That is the IMP.**

Instead, what we really need is a tool for summarizing the campaign's objective and driving forces, and our marketing approach for engaging the target audiences. We need an executive summary that we can use to share with internal executives to gain their approval. We also need a template that can be easily shared with members of the global marketing team to best prepare them for the execution phase. That way, we get everyone singing off the same hymnal.

Getting to Gate 1

As introduced in chapter 2, the objective of the Gate 1 review is to set forth the campaign strategy, including the estimated resource requirements necessary for success, **before** work actually begins on the campaign. It's worth repeating that countless hours and dollars have been lost in developing ad hoc marketing activities that later get cancelled or flat out miss their mark. Gate 1 is intended to help guide and reinforce team decisions so these precious resources are not wasted.

It is no coincidence that the table of contents for Part 1 of the IMP is the same as the agenda for the Gate 1 steering committee review meeting (see Figure 20).

In actuality, we already began working on the first few IMP sections in Chapter 3: campaign name & description, campaign objectives, and the overarching value proposition. Now let's drill down the campaign map.

```
Gate 1 Review Table of Contents

• Campaign name & description
• Campaign objective(s)
• Value proposition
• Campaign map
• Tactical calendar (program view only)
• Rough budget estimate
• Key assumptions
• Synergies with other campaigns
```

Figure 20: Table of Contents for the Gate 1 Review Meeting

Introducing the campaign map

With a clear understanding of our prioritized target market segments, the next questions are:

• What obstacles are stopping prospects from becoming customers? And, how can we help them overcome these obstacles by sharing specific information on their own terms?

• How can we best guide prospects through our sales cycle and encourage them to continually qualify themselves?

• What messages do we need to communicate to them, and in what sequence?

Marketers must carefully consider which marketing **programs** are best in addressing these questions in such a way that they help achieve the overall campaign objective(s).

The best marketing programs are centered not on discrete tactics (e.g., a Google adwords campaign, or a webinar). Instead, they are built around a specific marketing communications objective or theme. While there may be an unlimited number of marketing tactics available to marketers that could be part of any program, the basic marketing programs are thankfully few and easy for teams to rally around. Each company will select and tailor its programs using any combination of the following seven base program types:

- Awareness programs
- Competitive replacement programs
- Cross-sell/up-sell programs
- Migration programs
- New customer acquisition programs
- Nurture programs
- Renewal programs

These seven program types have been mapped against specific marketing communications objectives: awareness, interest, consideration, and buy/renew. (See Figure 21.) A campaign might have all program types represented within it, or it might have only a subset of these types. Also, a campaign may have multiple versions of several types. It is limited only by the creativity of the marketing team. Every marketing activity or offer produced should be nested within one of these seven program types. Doing so will help you stay focused on the dialog and the relationship you are building with your target audiences. To do otherwise will result in the fragmentation of your messages.

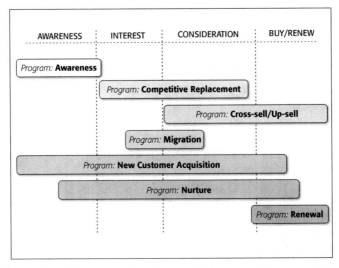

Figure 21: Mapping the Seven Program Types within a Campaign

Choosing the right programs

So, how many program types do you need? Must you use all seven? Can you have multiple versions of a program type within a campaign? And, how do you choose the right programs without immediately jumping to specific tactics? All excellent questions.

As marketing teams work through the IMP they will undoubtedly have hunches or expectations regarding what programs, activities, and offers will likely be appropriate. This can be very helpful in envisioning how the pieces of the campaign will ultimately come together. However, at this stage, we need to resist the temptation to dictate or prescribe specific actions (That will come soon enough after we have passed the Gate 1 review).

Instead, the purpose of the campaign map is to carefully scope the required program types necessary to achieve success of the campaign. Brainstorming on these questions is exactly what happens during the first synchronization meeting. For example, say we are launching a new product into the widget market. We know that IT system managers in enterprise businesses are our target audiences. We also know that competitor X is well entrenched, and that our company is not well known in this industry. What should our campaign map look like?

Based on this short description, the team will explore and debate alternatives for reaching these audiences. The goal is always on how to best build a relationship with these targets that encourages them to qualify themselves into or out of our sales funnel. Upon conclusion of the first synchronization meeting, the team might hypothesize the need for the following programs:

- **Awareness** – a thought leadership program designed to promote our company as a credible player in this industry and a safe choice as a trusted business partner

- **Awareness** – new widget launch program making use of carefully targeted PR, analyst, and viral marketing efforts

- **Competitive Replacement** – a program aimed at showing a side-by-side comparison of our product versus Competitor X's in specific use cases

- **New Customer Acquisition** – a program aimed at users who are not in Competitor X's installed base

Rather than worry about all the specific details within each program, the focus on the campaign map is, literally, to map out which programs are needed, in some logical order, to build a dialog with our intended market segment. In this case, we've hypothesized the need for four programs, two of which are awareness programs, which comprise the initial campaign (see Figure 22).

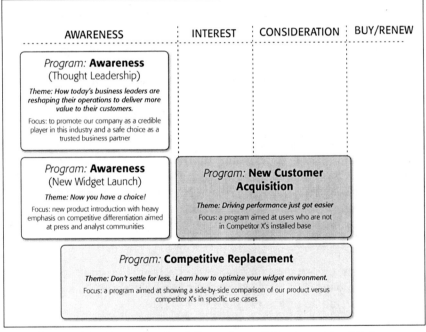

Figure 22: Hypothetical Mapping of Programs within a Campaign

The beauty of this map is that it is easy to understand and share with others. In one slide we can paint a picture that describes how the team's marketing efforts would be put to use. There will be many activities and offers (and all sort of tactics and deliverables) required to execute this campaign, but, we don't need to list them here. For now, we want to communicate the direction of our campaign and the strategy behind it.

But just listing programs on a page is not enough. Notice the short descriptors included in each program box in Figure 22. The marketing team must share the reasoning behind this recommended campaign map during the Gate 1 campaign strategy review to the steering committee. They must be able to define and describe in some detail what each program is, why it is needed, and what its specific objective(s) will be. The marketer also needs to carefully link each program back to a marketing communications objective (awareness, interest, consideration, or buy/renew). That way, it will be crystal clear how the programs link to each other.

Three common traps to avoid

- The *"More is Better"* trap: Many marketers fall into the trap of assuming that every product deserves its own campaign or program. One marketing team I worked with came to the conclusion they needed 251 unique programs! Much more than they could ever hope to possibly execute. More is not better. Even if the team had the depth of resources and dollars to produce and promote 251 programs, the target audience would be instantly inundated, confused, and likely angry at the "attack" upon them.

  The solution to getting out of this trap is to put the customer and their problem, not the product, at the center of marketing mix. By taking the product marketing managers' egos out of the mix, they saw how they could promote a comprehensive solution (made up of multiple products and services). The result: a 90% reduction of the initially proposed programs. Promoting a manageable set of awareness, new customer acquisition, competitive replacement, and renewal programs around this solution set became instantly more manageable and whole lot less overwhelming.

  Marketing Truism #1: It is better to be wildly successful on fewer programs than fail miserably on many.

- **The "Functional Silo Program" trap:** On the other extreme, occasionally marketers will gravitate to developing programs based on the marketing functions (e.g., a PR program or a direct marketing program). However, in the context of developing the IMP, the key word in integrated. World-class integrated marketing programs link press releases to case studies and direct mails to blogs and YouTube videos to websites, and so on. Customers and prospects don't experience the world one marketing function at a time. When it comes to developing an IMP, marketers need to overtly tie their activities across media types, while at the same time producing their deliverables in a smart, productive way.

Marketing Truism #2: Artful marketing is like leaving a trail of bread crumbs easy for the prospect to follow.

- **The "Campaign Silo" trap:** A little rivalry and competition between campaign managers can be a good thing if it results in higher quality campaign strategies and plans. However, when competition (or ignorance) produces isolated campaigns, companies miss opportunities for leverage or create gaps in messaging that can confuse the market.

During my tenure as a campaign manager at both HP and Sun, we worked hard to avoid this trap. We made it a point to have all the campaign managers meet weekly or every other week to update each other on our campaign status so we could explore overlaps and gaps and make trade-offs. These meetings were sometimes formal and structured; other times they were informal and casual. The point was to establish a forum where we could learn from each other and be reminded of how our campaigns fit together. There is no question that these sessions helped us build a strong camaraderie and optimize our campaigns at the same time.

Marketing Truism #3: The best campaign managers are business managers, always looking out for the greater good and willing to make compromises and trade-offs.

The high-level tactical calendar

Once we've identified the recommended programs, the next step is to lay them against a timeline. Figure 23 presents an operational tactical plan, albeit at a high level.

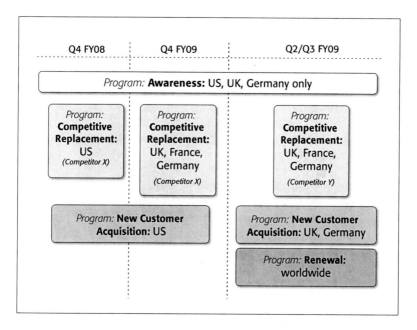

Figure 23: An Example of a High-level Tactical Calendar

This step is where many teams struggle. When most marketers are asked to think tactically, they are immediately drawn into the minutia. There is a great temptation to lay out every detail of every tactic and action item. That is not what is needed at this stage of the IMP development.

Instead, our intent is to show in a simple timeline when the programs will be executed. Will a program be managed in a multi-phase approach? Which quarter will phase 1 be executed? Which programs will span multiple quarters? Mapping a high level tactical calendar helps management understand where resources and budget will need to be committed. We don't yet know all the details of who needs to do what and when. Once the IMP has been approved, the team will be given the "green light" to focus on those details. But focusing on them prematurely (i.e., before the programs have been approved) is a waste of time and energy.

Forecasting is always a tricky business. I've found that asking teams to focus mainly on the next two quarters, with some placeholders for the two quarters following, produces more meaningful and realistic results, rather than requiring full details for an entire year. Here are a few tips for sketching out a high-level tactical calendar:

- Think in terms of a whole year, but give weighting to a rolling six-month window

- Once the plan is approved, this tactical calendar should be updated quarterly

- Stay within the budget guidelines you've been given; however, think beyond the budget: consider non-budget resource requirements

- Coordinate the timing against that of other campaigns

- Be mindful of real-world events and competitive moves that may impact your campaign

This is very important: keep in mind that the context for this tactical calendar is within the Gate 1 review meeting. It presents an expectation of resources that will be required to successfully execute the campaign. Be realistic and pragmatic. If there are obstacles or concerns that will impact the ability to successfully execute the plan, then these issues need to be shared with the steering committee. The high-level tactical calendar is a tool for sharing this expectation.

Rough budget estimate

One of the most common challenges for any team developing a campaign is to forecast the necessary budget. Occasionally, a team will be stymied believing that a detailed budget must be given to them before they can begin planning. Avoid the temptation to wallow in frustration. Let us assume that we will never have all the money we would like. Therefore, there will always be a need to prioritize our marketing efforts. Yes, we do need to be practical in making sure that our recommendations fit within an available budget. But at the same time, it is the campaign's team duty to recommend what is needed to ensure success with these strategic campaigns. It has been my experience that when something is critically important and supported with strong evidence, available budget can be found. We can keep this in mind as we develop our plan.

The budgeting process starts with the prospect/customer in mind. Our goal is to move the prospect through the sales cycle. To that end, we know what programs will be needed, as we have already described. Based on our experiences and our knowledge of the marketplace, we should be able to come up with a reasonable budget estimate to ensure success. Obviously, this number will have a wide plus or minus variance, because we haven't yet specified the details. However, there are a few places you can go to get some good insights:

1. **Consider what your company spent last year on marketing campaigns and programs.** Although these campaigns and programs may have been treated differently than we have prescribed in this book, an analysis of past spending behaviors will give you a good place to base a practical estimate.

2. **Ask outside agencies and consultants for budget estimates for similar campaigns and programs, as we have defined them in this book.** Although all campaigns and programs are unique, the general cost can be estimated fairly well. For example, a professionally run and facilitated Customer Advisory Board program (i.e., Nurture Program) will cost a company anywhere between $150K–$250K annually. A six-month awareness campaign run through print, online, and television media can easily cost several million dollars. Ask the experts to give you an "order of magnitude" budget estimate.

3. **Search the Internet.** There is a huge library of articles and blogs on marketing planning and budgeting. Some quick research can provide enough details to base your rough estimate.

Tips for managing the budget process

- For best results, management should be able to provide some general guidance on the range of spend in order to help the campaign teams scope their programs appropriately. If they can't, do the best you can to document a set of reasonable assumptions so you can easily describe your logic when presenting your budget recommendation.

- The budgeting process is part art and part science. Spreadsheets will tell you only so much. You must also plan for the unplannable. Make sure you pad your numbers to cover unforeseen events. It is easier to reduce a project's scope than to ask for more money later.

- Campaign managers who arbitrarily dictate the budget end up alienating team members. Avoid this temptation. Instead, they should facilitate this discussion, but not dictate or prescribe the final recommendation. This needs to be a team-based recommendation.

- Global and regional marketing representatives need to work together to estimate the budget and resources requirements for their programs in their regions. These estimates can then be added to produce a comprehensive global budget estimate.

- Be clear in setting budget estimate expectations. The Gate 1 budget estimate will likely include a variance as much as +/-100%. The Gate 2 budget estimate is expected to be much more detailed with a much smaller variance. A good budget range would be +/-20%.

- Expect that the budget will continue to be tightened and refined as the team moves from the planning mode into the execution mode.

- Don't let the budget discussion hinder creative ideas and exploring new ways to bring messages to the market.

Documenting assumptions and identifying synergies

This last piece of the first half of the IMP, and an equally important part of the Gate 1 review meeting, is an acknowledgment of the assumptions and synergies the team has made in producing the campaign map.

Because the IMP is created using imperfect information, it is understood that assumptions need to be made. This section documents any major assumptions that, if proven incorrect, could have a major positive or negative impact on the campaign. Assumptions are usually segmented into the three types:

* Key assumptions about the target audience

  Example: Target audience priorities are based on the observation that CIOs in banks and retail industries are early adopters of Product X.

* Key assumptions about the campaign and how long it should last

  Example: Email and presence at industry events are the most effective avenues for reaching our target audience.

  Example: Because the average decision process takes 9–12 months, our campaign requires constant presence for 18 months to ensure best results.

* Key assumptions about our company's ability to execute the campaign

  Example: Marketing resources will be reallocated from Project Y in December to ensure a smooth rollout. Based on using only the current available resources, the rollout would be delayed until March.

A word about presenting to the steering committee at Gate 1

You've now completed the first draft of the IMP. You've set your strategy, crafted a recommendation for your programs, and estimated the resources required to ensure success. Whether you are a CMO, campaign team member, or a representative on the steering committee, here are a few suggestions on how to make this meeting the most productive.

Helpful tips for the campaign team members:

- Before you make your presentation, it is always a good idea to pre-sell your recommendations to steering committee members, especially the ones who are likely to disagree. By sharing your recommendations early and proactively incorporating their feedback, you will expedite the Gate 1 approval process. Steering committee members appreciate this, and so will you.

- Present your recommendation professionally with conviction. Although steering committee meetings can sometime be intimidating, speak with passion and with authority. You and your team are the experts of your campaign, not the steering committee.

- The steering committee is not interested in the details. Focus your presentation on the most important aspects of the campaign and on where you need their guidance or involvement to remove obstacles.

- Be prepared. Have a crisp, clean presentation, including handouts for all steering committee members. And, have the data to defend your recommendations if quizzed about the details. If you are not prepared, the steering committee will eat you for lunch.

- Formatting tips:

  - If you have a 60 minute presentation, plan for 30 minutes of slides, and 30 minutes of Q&A.

  - Font size must be greater than 18 point type. A tip for the presenter is to print out each slide, place it on the floor and try to read it while standing directly over it. If you can't read it, the type is too small.

  - Share tables and graphics in hardcopy if they are too hard to read in presentation format.

  - Your handouts can be detailed, but don't expect the steering committee members to read them.

- Don't be alarmed if you don't receive Gate 1 approval at the first steering committee meeting. The steering committee, having access to all campaigns, will likely have feedback and additional requirements you haven't considered. Take this feedback in stride; regroup with your campaign team and make the updates in time for the next meeting.

Helpful tips for the steering committee representatives:

- If provided with the campaign strategy slides before the meeting, make the time to peruse them. This will help you understand the material and quickly work through the discussion.

- Ask questions. The worst steering committee meetings are when members are distracted or not engaged. This is a disservice to yourself and the campaign team.

- Set the team up for success by ensuring that the campaign objectives are:
  - Understood correctly and completely
  - Sponsored and backed by the appropriate executives
  - Achievable

- Provide constructive criticism. It's easy to be an unhelpful critic. But, the best steering committee sessions I've attended are the ones where the members voiced concerns or disagreements clearly with specific feedback so the campaign team understood what action they needed to take.

- Acknowledge good work. Campaign teams are made up of people who have worked hard to bring their recommendations to you. If they have done a good job and are well prepared, let them know.

5 Working the Process: Part 2 – Creating Program Blueprints

We don't want to create a "scattershot" of seemingly random messaging and tactics. Instead, we want to deploy a cohesive sustained, relevant dialog with a target prospect. To do this, we need a program blueprint. Chapter 5 describes this part of the process in detail, including the introduction of the "program blueprints" for seven of the most common types of programs.

"Good fortune is what happens when opportunity meets planning."[9]
Thomas Alva Edison, inventor

Getting to Gate 2

As we discussed in Chapter 4, the Gate 1 review is used to confirm the campaign strategy. Once the steering committee has approved the general approach, the team can now begin to sort out the details that will make up the programs. Defining and prioritizing program details, activities, and offers is far easier to do with a confirmed campaign strategy than without one. The activi-

9. Thinkexist.com, http://tinyurl.com/34ceks.

ties and offers within each program can be laid out in a blueprint fashion. Just as in laying out plumbing and electrical fixtures when designing a house, a program blueprint is a tool used to show how all the various marketing vehicles fit together to support the campaign. Thought of another way, the program blueprint displays a "trail of bread crumbs" intended to engage the prospect in a relevant, meaningful dialog and guide them quickly through or out of the sales cycle.

Development and agreement on the program details will require several synchronization meetings with the global team. No doubt program trade-offs will be required in order to decide on the optimum marketing mix. And the campaign managers must be mindful of synergies, overlaps, and gaps between their campaign and campaigns run by their peers. All of these discussions will ultimately culminate in the presentation of program recommendations shared with the steering committee at the Gate 2 review.

The purpose of the Gate 2 review is to confirm these program priorities as well as expectations and resources required for successful execution. Again, it is not a coincidence that the table of contents for Part 2 of the IMP is the same as the agenda for the Gate 2 review (see Figure 24).

Gate 2 Review Table of Contents

- Summary of revisions from Gate 1 meeting
- Overview of key program blueprints
  - Program executive summaries
    - Program name, description, objective
    - Program blueprints (showing the connections between activities and offers)
    - Program calendar of major events
- Synergies with other campaigns and/or programs
- Open issues requiring steering committee guidance

Figure 24: Table of Contents for the Gate 2 Review Meeting

The logic behind program blueprints

Programs are about achieving a specific marketing result through the use of a series of marketing activities and offers. The program objectives, coupled with specific insight into understanding how the target audience wants to be communicated with, will guide the team's recommendation for the optimum marcom mix.

Blueprints are the key because they provide a structure for us to use to map out this interaction. During the course of this dialog we can and will:

- reinforce messages,

- engage prospects and customers on their own terms, and

- help prospects and customers buy when they are ready to buy (not when we are ready to sell).

The fact of the matter is that most marketing communications being executed today contain messages irrelevant to the target audience. Our job is to focus our messaging on things that matter most to the audience, when they are ready to hear them. The objective is to "personalize" the dialog and the timing to the needs of individuals and to sustain that communication over time and across multiple media and sales channels. If we can think through this process and capture our thoughts in a blueprint, our ability to achieve success will increase dramatically.

Fortunately for marketers, there are really only seven primary program building blocks. (See Figure 25, and refer to Appendix C for additional examples of each of the blueprint types.) They are carefully designed to move prospects through (or out of) the sales funnel. Using the building block concept marketers are forced to focus on the objective of their programs before jumping to tactics. This is an essential discipline associated with the most effective marketing teams. Although there are only seven program types, there can be an unlimited number of ways they can be executed. For example, awareness programs might take the guise of a "general brand awareness" program through advertising, or a "thought leadership" program with a heavy focus on executive speaking events, or even a "corporate sponsorships" program with visibility at sports arenas or events. In this case, the umbrella program objective is awareness, yet the focus of that awareness is different within the application of each program. This gives marketers complete license for creativity but within a disciplined program structure.

The seven program blueprint types

- Awareness programs
- Competitive replacement programs
- Cross-sell/up-sell programs
- Migration programs
- New customer acquisition programs
- Nurture programs
- Renewal programs

Figure 25: Tying Programs to a Specific Marketing or Sales Objective

Unfortunately, marketers sometimes confuse activities as being programs. Figure 26 lists a few common marketing misinterpretations.

Activities are not Programs

The following are activities that may be part of a larger program. They should not be thought of as stand-alone programs in and of themselves.

- Press releases
- Google adwords
- Search engine optimization
- Direct mail
- Advertising

We will only know if these activities are optimal if we understand how and when they fit together to create the dialog we want with the target audience.

Figure 26: Understanding the Difference between Activities Versus Programs

Marketers will occasionally jump to a conclusion that a specific activity is required and that the activity, because of its importance, constitutes its own program. This is short-sighted thinking because it suggests that the activity is independent of any other marketing activity.

For example, press releases, editorials, and placement of feature articles are extremely important elements of a marketing mix. But, it is a piece of the whole. We need to realign our communications efforts and look at our marketing deliverables in the same way the customer sees and experiences them – as a flow of information.

Examining a few blueprint examples

Perhaps the best way to understand blueprints is to look at a few examples. Figure 27 illustrates a program designed to acquire new customers. Because this complete process can be lengthy, the illustration specifies that this example is for phase 1. Other phases may overlap or extend this model, depending on the specific market or business issues faced by the marketing team. Notice that the target audience is listed on the left-hand side of the chart. The marketing communications objectives (awareness, interest, consideration) are at the top.

Each box represents a piece of the dialog. Each piece of the dialog has a theme around which the activity or offer will be based. In blueprint example #1, the dialog begins with sharing enterprise security best practices with CIOs. The first set of activities is represented as mechanisms that will invite CIOs to participate in a series of events to hear and collect this information. As this dialog continues to unfold, prospects will be invited to other activities and offers. It is critically important that these activities and offers are linked in a logical sequence.

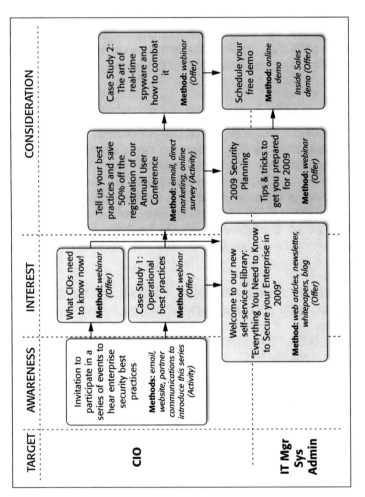

Figure 27: Example of a Blueprint for a New Customer Acquisition Program

Through the blueprint we are telling a story. To repeat an analogy I used earlier: think of this flow chart as a trail of bread crumbs designed to help lead a prospect through your sales process. This is a story about acquiring new customers. We've suggested that a good way to capture their interest is with an invitation to participate in a series of events to learn about enterprise security best practices. If the CIO engages, we can then point them to some additional resources (e.g., a second webinar or a case study). If they respond to that, we might direct them to a new e-library. Only after they have attended or participated in a prior event do we consider them a serious lead. The activities noted under "consideration" would likely include more interaction from the sales team.

Figure 28 shows another example of a new customer acquisition program. This example starts with awareness activities that prepare their target audience to receive a trialware offer. Once that offer has been received and evaluated, follow-up steps and offers are initiated to encourage the prospect to purchase a complete solution. Notice the role that inside sales and sales teams play within the activities listed in the blueprint. It is quite common for marketing teams to forget to include the sales force as a channel for communicating messages and offers.

The same approach shown in these two examples can be applied with each of the other six blueprint types. They all start with careful prospect targeting, and then map out a sequence of activities and offers from which to build a dialog and a relationship. Designing a blueprint can be challenging, especially if the marketers are individual contributors who's job it is to be concerned about all the details. However, with a bit of direction and coaching from marketing leaders and campaign managers, the team will perform better by keeping an eye on the big picture. Blueprints are the table of contents of the marketing story. The tactics will follow in a detailed tactical plan that will be developed upon Gate 2 approval.

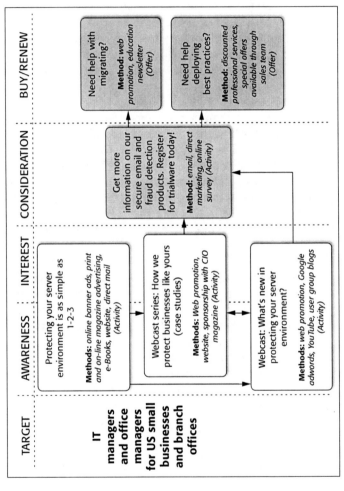

TARGET	AWARENESS	INTEREST	CONSIDERATION	BUY/RENEW
IT managers and office managers for US small businesses and branch offices	Protecting your server environment is as simple as 1-2-3 **Methods:** *online banner ads, print and on-line magazine advertising, e-Books, website, direct mail (Activity)*	Webcast series: How we protect businesses like yours (case studies) **Methods:** *Web promotion, website, sponsorship with CIO magazine (Activity)* Webcast: What's new in protecting your server environment? **Methods:** *web promotion, Google adwords, YouTube, user group blogs (Activity)*	Get more information on our secure email and fraud detection products. Register for trialware today! **Method:** *email, direct marketing, online survey (Activity)*	Need help with migrating? **Method:** *web promotion, education newsletter (Offer)* Need help deploying best practices? **Method:** *discounted professional services, special offers available through sales team (Offer)*

Figure 28: A Second Example of a Blueprint for a New Customer Acquisition Program

Questions you must be able to answer before you can build a program blueprint

If you are like most marketers, you are eager to take action. But, what is the right action to take? Uncounted dollars and time are wasted when marketers follow the "ready, fire, aim" approach. But, leaders can help their teams most by asking six key questions before pulling the trigger on any program (see Figure 29). Let's look at them one at a time.

Six Key Questions for Program Design

1. Who is the target audience?
2. How do they want to be communicated with?
3. What offers do they want/expect from us?
4. After they respond to the first activity and offer, what happens next? And what happens after that?
5. What happens if they don't respond?
6. How will your activities and offers help qualify prospects?

Figure 29: Key Program Design Questions

1) Who is the target audience?

The answer to this question begins in the customer set discussion we had in Chapter 3. When we defined a customer set, we focused on an actual group of customers for a given type of offering who have a common set of needs and who reference each other. But, when it comes to tailoring a specific program, we need to peel the onion a bit further.

The fact of the matter is that we will graciously sell our product to anyone and everyone who wishes to purchase it. However, our marketing dollars and time are limited. Thus, we must be highly focused in where, when, and how we will proactively market our wares. We can think of our target customer set as a literal target, where concentric rings represent different sub-segments. The final question really is *who is in the bull's eye?* Which sub-segment is most important, most likely to buy? Perhaps they represent a beachhead in a new market or country. The more focused we can be, the more relevant we can tailor our dialog, and the higher ROI we will achieve from the program.

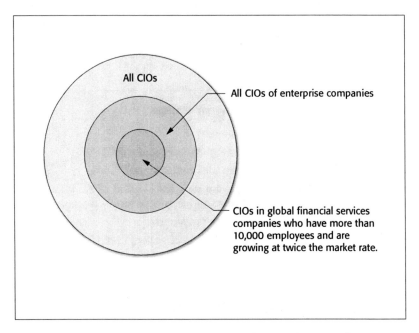

Figure 30: Targeting Prospects Means Aiming for the Bull's Eye

An example: When I ask this question, I most often get a response like, "CIOs are our target audience." Okay. This is good, but it is not enough for our purposes. Not all CIOs are created equal. Do CIOs of telecommunications companies think the same as CIOs of small businesses? Do CIOs in Germany worry about the same things as CIOs in Japan? A better answer to the question might be something like what is shown in Figure 30:

Our target is CIOs in global financial services companies who have more than 10,000 employees and are growing at twice the market rate.

Or, another example might be:

Our target is radiologists in US hospitals in the six most rapidly growing cities who are already looking to phase out traditional x-ray technology in favor of digital radiography solutions.

As you can see, in each example, we've focused by providing more details, more adjectives to carefully fine-tune who we want to reach. Undoubtedly, other fringe audiences will hear our messages. This is fine. And, if they respond, so much the better. However, our best chance to cut through the marketplace noise is to be as focused as possible so we can take our best shot.

2) How do they want to be communicated with?

Before we jump into action, we should take a moment to put ourselves in the prospect's shoes. They are busy people, bombarded with too much information (most of it irrelevant). Today's customers and prospects are very savvy and want to control what information they receive and when they receive it. This is the era of opt-in marketing and personal one-on-one engagement. We must respect their preferences. Ignore them, and you will be relegated to the junk mail bin. So, how do we decide upon the optimal marcom mix?

To begin to answer that question, take a look at your current installed base. Talk with them to understand what sources of information they commonly refer to when evaluating vendors and solutions. How are they interacting with you now, and how would they prefer to interact with you? Is there a difference? Also, look at how your competitors are communicating. What innovative things are they doing to engage the prospect in a meaningful, relevant dialogue?

Fortunately and unfortunately for marketers, technology is creating new channels for us get our messages in front of prospects and customers. YouTube, MySpace, and blogs are just the latest tools that are challenging the concept of a traditional marcom mix. Talk to prospects at tradeshows and industry events, not just about your products or services, but about how they like to be communicated with and what types of information they are most interested in. Give the prospect multiple avenues to collect information and let them decide which ones work best for them. Invite them to engage you on their own terms.

3) What offers do they want/expect from us?

This is all about producing a relevant dialog with the intended audience. Just because you have whitepaper, does it mean you should offer it to everyone in your target audience? Only do so if it is relevant, containing information they value. Marketers often fall into the trap of offering what they have versus offering what prospects and customers value. World-class marketers understand the difference.

This is another opportunity to understand that "more is not necessarily better." When it comes to helping a prospect through a sales cycle, one relevant, focused whitepaper offered at the right time will be valued much more than 10 articles thrown at them randomly.

As a rule of thumb, any offers we make must be:

- **Carefully targeted:** It should address the target reader as an individual, not a mass market.

- **Engaging:** It must have a focused message and not a confusing, random collection of all possible messages. Want to better your chances? Make the offer intriguing, fun, even entertaining.

- **Relevant:** It must contain information that is pertinent to their decision process.

- **Meaningful:** It must contain logical, substantiated, clearly written information that is easy to read and understand.

- **Timely:** It must come to the reader's attention when they are ready and interested in receiving it.

Miss any one of these, and the lead generation conversion rates will fall greatly.

4) After they respond to the first activity, what happens next?

Our goal is not just to sell a product or service. We want to engage the prospect in an ongoing dialog that becomes the basis for a relationship. We want to build customer loyalty now – not just at the close of a sale. Unfortunately, it is sadly true that most marketing teams are so busy in executing a specific activity or event that the follow-up is sorely lacking.

Examples of disconnected activities:

- The marketing team rigorously works the details in executing a grand tradeshow event and capturing 1,000 leads. But the leads sit on a desk for two weeks before being entered into a sales force automation (SFA) system for follow-up.

- A webinar is conducted to promote a new product. The event concludes without a call to action. Worse, for the fifty prospects who attend, there is not a follow-up thank you email or an invitation to check out other resources that may be of interest to them.

- A product launch complete with press activity and print advertising is executed, but the sales team is unaware of the launch until they hear about it from their customers.

- A Customer Advisory Board is held in a scenic location and generates high energy and expectations with customers. Yet, the thank you email and executive summary report acknowledging next steps never is delivered.

Relationships are based on trust and are the foundation for creating customer loyalty. Just as in playing a good game of chess, we want to think one, two, or three moves ahead so we can best anticipate the prospect's needs for information. Every marketing activity needs to overtly link to the next so the prospect knows where she should go next. This lack of follow-through happens all the time. Don't let it happen to you.

5) What happens if they don't respond?

One of a marketer's worst fears is in hosting an event but no one showing up. To alleviate this fear, the careful marketer must consider actions for those prospects who chose not to (or cannot) engage at this time. The reasons for a lack of response may be many: poor messaging, unfocused target audience, improper offers, bad timing. In each case, the marketer needs to have a plan of action to follow up and give the audience another chance to engage. A few obvious but often missed options include:

- Sending a "sorry we missed you" email with an invitation to visit the next event.

- Creating a "nurture" list – a list of all opt-in prospects who have not engaged. Send gentle reminders to them, inviting them to take advantage of other information resources and to participate in future events.

- Resending the direct mail piece but with a different offer.

- Having an inside sales rep call to check in with them and follow-up.

Marketers should always be testing different offers, messages, and vehicles to see what works best. If at first we don't succeed, we need to alter a variable or two and try again. It's easy to get frustrated, but keep the faith. The more we understand what approach works best with our target audiences, the more effective our programs will be.

6) How will your activities and offers help qualify prospects?

Bottom line: Marketing and sales must be working with a "hand in glove" mentality in order to achieve optimum success. Unfortunately, many organizations seem to treat marketing and sales teams as competing organizations. Sales demands more leads; but marketing wants to know what happened to the leads they gave sales last quarter. This adversarial relationship hurts companies and alienates customers and prospects.

Marketing exists to help sales close deals. That's all that really matters. Whether it be through advertising programs or webinars or whatever, a good marketer works closely with sales to determine what volume and types of leads are needed. Then, marketers can design and execute the marketing programs to best deliver them. To do this, each marketing activity requires a careful call-to-action that will encourage a prospect to advance themselves through the sales cycle or out of it.

If we know that a prospect has visited our website three times last month and attended a recent webinar, then we can assume some sincere interest in our product or service. This is likely a high quality lead. If, on the other hand, a prospect signed up for a webinar but didn't attend, we might offer him a second chance to engage with us. Marketers will want to nurture this lead over time. And, it should never be handed to sales unless or until it satisfies pre-defined qualification criteria.

Designing your own blueprints

Only you and your team can develop the right program blueprint for your business. However, to help you get started, I've included generic templates for the seven basic program types that you can build from in Appendix C. Use these as your starting point to explore how activities and offers like these can be linked for best results.

Again, don't worry about the myriad of details of who does what on Tuesday and how the activities will eventually be managed. For now, the purpose of the blueprint exercise is to build the structure of the ongoing dialog between you and your target prospect. Tips to get you started:

- Match your program blueprints to how your customers buy your products, not how your company's marketing and sales teams are currently organized. Remember: the target customer is the center of your universe.

- Test the programs, activities, offers and refine them in real time.

- Build in a feedback loop to optimize the activities and offers that make up each program.

- Measure success or failure of activities and offers often. Understanding why a marketing program fails can be the most important thing a marketer can learn.

- Don't forget to measure conversion rates between activities and offers.

- Don't be afraid to make changes in "mid-flight." Variables that can change include calls to action, offers, marketing mix, and messaging.

Program blueprint critique sheet

The blueprint is not an execution plan. As you brainstorm your own blueprints, here's a quick critique sheet to keep you on track.

- Focus, focus, focus: do the activities and offers in your blueprint support the campaign and program objectives?

- Is each activity and offer appropriate for your designated target audience?

- Are next steps logically addressed?
  - What happens next if a prospect responds?
  - What happens next if they don't?

- What is the optimum marketing mix that supports the program?
  - Are you leveraging the right marketing media?
  - At the right time?
  - In the right geographies/regions?

- Is your program realistic, based on your company's history, the likely ability to execute it, and the availability of budget and resources?

Remember, program blueprints are not . . .

- A long list of every activity and offer you could possibly provide to a prospect
  More is NOT better

- A list of random, unconnected activities and offers.
  Each succeeding step must build off of the prior step.

- Focused on a single point in time
  Instead, they guide a prospect through the sales cycle

- A tactical execution plan filled with action items, owners, and due dates
  The tactical execution plan is built after the IMP has been approved

6 Choosing Proper Metrics

One of the most common points of confusion is in choosing the proper metrics on which to base a campaign's success. Chapter 6 shares terminology and best practices for understanding cascading metrics and building an appropriate scorecard for any campaign.

"Being able to "crunch the numbers" is vital to success in marketing. Knowing which numbers to crunch, however, is a skill that develops over time." [10]

Paul W. Farris, from his book "Marketing Metrics – 50+ Metrics Every Executive Should Master"

---

10. Paul W. Farris, *Marketing Metrics - 50+ Metrics Every Executive Should Master*, Warton School Publishing, 2006; BrandNexus Book Reviews, www.brandnexus.com/book_reviews.php.

Understanding metrics

Before we can decide which metrics are most appropriate to track and measure, we need to go back to the campaign objective. We introduced the concept of a "campaign-level" marketing objective in Chapter 3, defining this as the umbrella objective in the following way:

> *Once all the marketing programs, activities, and offers have been run, what have we achieved?*

Of course, this description is like looking in the rear-view mirror to know where we've been. We need to be more forward-thinking in our approach to setting effective marketing objectives and metrics. To do this, every marketer at every level must understand the business goals and objectives because these will drive their choice of which metrics are the most appropriate. Unfortunately, separating campaign-level metrics from tactical metrics is a common challenge for most marketers.

Figure 31 offers a perspective on how our cascading objectives fit together. A company's business goal always resides at the top. This is the impetus against which the marketing team, and all other departments, needs to align their plans. These goals will ultimately guide our behavior as well as the definition of our campaigns and programs.

Directly underneath the business goal is where our campaign objective resides. Underneath that, we will have the various program objectives that support our campaign. Whereas the campaign's objective should be a single objective broad in scope, the program objectives may be many and more narrowly scoped. And, finally, underneath the program objectives are the many tactical marketing activities and offers needed to comprise the programs. Although every marketing activity may also carry its own set of metrics, it is important not to get too tangled and overwhelmed with metrics. We must avoid the point where *analysis paralysis* invades our thinking and sucks us into the black hole of indecision.

Figure 31: A Model for Cascading Marketing Objectives

When I asked one marketing director about his campaign-level objectives, he responded by telling me his objectives were the following:

- To generate 12 press releases, one per month

- To launch a new website in September

- To generate 1,200 leads

- To implement Google adwords

- To update collateral pieces by March

- To hire a new director of marketing before the next board meeting

Unfortunately, none of these are true, meaningful campaign-level objectives. Rather, they are a mix of operating tactics and isolated metrics that can be checked off a to-do list. This is not what we are really looking for.

Figure 32 provides an example of cascading metrics. As you can see, each succeeding step offers more specifics and granularity on the metrics that follow. These metrics move from being strategic to being tactical. Development of the most meaningful and relevant metrics can be difficult.

An Example of Cascading Metrics

1. Business goal: to generate $100M this fiscal year

2. Campaign objective and associated metric: To grow North American market-share by 15% within 18 months

3. Program objective and associated metric: To launch an aggressive competitive replacement program aimed at competitor Y's installed base and convert 500 new customers in Q3.

4. Activities and associated metrics:

   a. Sales development activities: use our inside sales team to mine competitor Y's installed base, producing 150 new contacts and 15 new leads per month beginning in April.

   b. Whitepaper promotion: Generate more than 500 web hits per month via the promotion of a new independent competitive comparison report showing use cases and results of our product versus competitor Y's product (New whitepaper to be offered via the web and printed collateral).

Figure 32: An Example of Linking Goals and Objectives to Appropriate Metrics

Here are a few tips that have helped marketing teams.

1. **Track only those metrics that will help you make decisions:** The simple fact is that most metrics are irrelevant or overkill. The trick is to focus on only those metrics that will help you and your team optimize decision making. In addition to tracking marketing performance metrics, make it a priority to understand your sales pipeline model. Measuring conversion rates between stages in the pipeline can be an important leading indicator of where you need to focus your marketing efforts in the future. But remember, just because you can track a metric, doesn't mean that you should or that having that information is worth the investment it costs you to track it.

2. **Avoid getting caught in the weeds:** The easiest place to start generating metrics is also the most dangerous. That is to say that when the individual marketing media managers generate their own metrics out of context with the business goal and campaign-level objectives, the result is a mish-mash of tactical items that may or may not be relevant and appropriate. Your search for the most relevant metrics should always start at the campaign-level and work their way downstream; not the other way around.

3. **Avoid the "more is better" trap:** Occasionally, marketing teams attempt to brainstorm their way into deciding the metrics they will use. Although brainstorming is often a very good technique to encourage creative thinking, it can lead to a lengthy list of all possible metrics. There is a point of diminishing returns when it comes to metrics management. Avoid the trap of analysis paralysis.

4. **Choosing between what is easy and what is right:** Oftentimes, I see marketing teams default to what metrics they already have or can easily generate. But, these may not be the best metrics to use. For example, it's hard to count press impressions, but easy to count the number of press releases. I was amazed to find one marketing VP attempt to substantiate their results by directly equating sales to the number of press releases generated. (Seasoned press relations managers will cringe when I say that this VP was also dismissive of any criteria relating to newsworthiness.) To be fair, his team was executing other

marketing programs with other metrics, but the number of press releases was his "bell weather" metric. Not surprisingly, his tenure as VP of the corporate marketing team was short-lived.

The importance of a scorecard

But how do you really know what you should be measuring? And what is a proper benchmark to be measured against? This numeric imperative represents a significant challenge. In business and economics, many metrics are complex and difficult to master. Some are highly specialized and best suited to specific analyses. Many require data that may be approximate, incomplete, or unavailable. Under these circumstances, no single metric is likely to be perfect.

For this reason, I recommend that marketers use a portfolio or "scorecard" approach to metrics management. By doing so, they can view market dynamics from various perspectives and arrive at "triangulated" insights and perspectives. Additionally, with multiple metrics, marketers can use each as a check on the others. In this way, they can maximize the accuracy of their knowledge. They can also estimate or project one data point on the basis of others. Of course, to use multiple metrics effectively, marketers must appreciate the relationship between them and the limitations inherent in each. When this understanding is achieved, however, metrics can help a marketing team maintain a productive focus on customers and markets.

Metrics, like the ones shown in a mock marketing scorecard in Figure 33 can help managers identify the strengths and weaknesses in both strategies and execution. In looking at this example, we might conclude that the marketing pipeline is in a bit of trouble: the number of quarterly responses has decreased the last two quarters; however, it looks like the response-lead conversion rate may have improved slightly in Q3 and Q4. Regardless, the number of opportunities looks rather thin. But keep in mind that numbers only tell us part of the story. We also need to know the reasons behind the numbers. Factors such as seasonality, economic and political events, as well as competitive threats and our own ability to execute marketing campaigns will influence the numbers. We need to know why. Only then, will we know what we need to do.

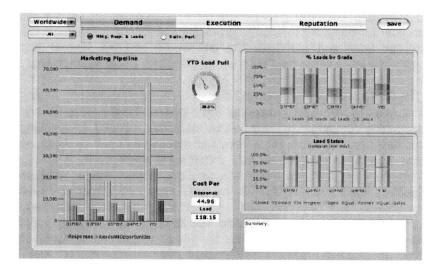

Figure 33: An Example of a Mock Marketing Scorecard

Mathematically defined and widely disseminated, metrics can become part of a precise, operational language within a marketing and sales organization. Most of all, dashboards and scorecards are meant to be shared with management as well as the rank-and-file. Make them visible. Talk about the implications behind the numbers. Use this tool to prompt discussion and the brainstorming of corrective actions to improve marketing results. Celebrate successes when they occur and rally the team when results show that programs fail to deliver. Although there are several generic tools that can be used for creating marketing dashboards and scorecards, the best results are attained when they are customized for your organization.

A case in point: Not long ago a CMO pulled me aside and expressed his frustration at a recent board meeting. During the meeting much of the angst was put on marketing's supposed inability to deliver leads to sales. He knew that plenty of good leads were being delivered, but without data to show where the leads had gone and how they were being acted upon by the sales department, it was too easy to point the finger at the marketing department. What was needed, he claimed, was a marketing dashboard that represented each marketing campaign and allowed management to drill down to track each lead against the eleven-stage sales pipeline. After six weeks of work customizing a marketing dashboard software program and kickstarting an internal marketing metrics program, the dashboard architecture was agreed upon and launched. The first weeks required manual data entry, but much of the data entry would eventually become automated.

The board meeting the following quarter went much differently. During this meeting, the CMO presented the dashboard highlighting several marketing campaigns and the number of leads produced. By mapping his dashboard with the sales force automation tool used by sales, he was able to track the lead flow through the sales cycle. It quickly became clear that the bottleneck was not in marketing's ability to produce leads. Instead, it lay in the sales reps' ability to quickly draft proposals. The creation and use of the marketing dashboard dramatically changed the agenda and tone of the following board meetings. Now, the CMO told me, the executive team could focus on the right problem areas.

As this example shows, marketing organizations are challenged to justify every activity and every dollar spent. It goes without saying that measuring the impact of marketing campaigns on customer acquisition, revenue and profitability is pivotal to the success of any good marketing organization. Unfortunately, closed-loop analysis can be hard work, because it involves correlating marketing data from campaign management platforms, manually-created spreadsheets, sales force automation tools, and other financial systems. Closing the loop requires analysis that straddles many disparate systems and data sources across the organization.

Luckily, managing and measuring marketing metrics is a popular topic on which there are a number of very good books, whitepapers, and resources available to assist you. (For example, see Paul W. Farris' *Marketing Metrics: 50+ Metrics Every Executive Should Master*, available on Amazon.com.) We won't duplicate that material here. But before you jump to building a home-grown metrics management system or engage with an outside consulting team, here are few key concepts that will help you create the most effective metrics framework.

Understanding the marketing knowledge hierarchy

Metrics management and reporting is only as good as the decisions it helps you make. To that end, the first questions we need to ask ourselves before embarking on a metrics program are the following:

1. **What questions do we need to be able to answer?** Because if we don't know what questions we need to answer, we'll spend too much time collecting metrics for the sake of collecting metrics.
2. **Who needs to know the answers and their implications?** Because if we provide the wrong answers to the wrong people, we confuse the real issues.
3. **Having received the answers and understood the implications, are we prepared to adjust our plans?** Because if we aren't prepared to act, we're just wasting our time.

These are weighty questions. How you answer them will directly affect the amount of time and energy you need to put into metrics management to be successful.

Start by constructing a marketing knowledge hierarchy, like the one shown in Figure 34. This hierarchy helps us understand who needs what type of information, in what detail, in what format, and how often. Ideally, data collection should be automated so reports at every level can be produced in real-time.

World-class marketing organizations understand that different people in a company require different levels of data in order to make the best business decisions. A CEO and her staff need a comprehensive marketing dashboard that up-levels all of marketing efforts. A series of simple graphics and charts that provide real-time insight on progress against the marketing objectives, and how they, in turn, impact the business objectives, works exceedingly well. Like the dashboard in your car, a marketing dashboard provides all the necessary dials and gauges to tell you where you are, where you're going and at what speed, along with indicator lights that illuminate at the first sign of a problem.

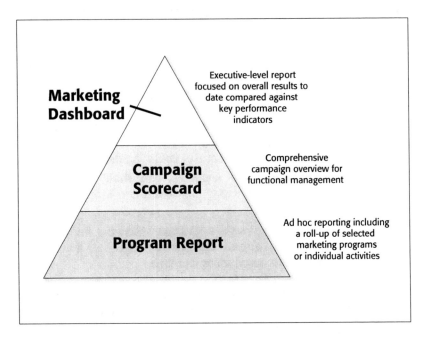

Marketing Dashboard — Executive-level report focused on overall results to date compared against key performance indicators

Campaign Scorecard — Comprehensive campaign overview for functional management

Program Report — Ad hoc reporting including a roll-up of selected marketing programs or individual activities

Figure 34: A Marketing Knowledge Hierarchy

Examples of executive-level dashboard features include the following:

- Aggregate marketing index depicting overall marketing success including the direct linkage between marketing activities and offers and the sales pipeline

- Quantifiable marketing ROI

- Identification of what campaigns and programs are doing better than expected

- Identification of what campaigns and programs are not performing well

- Predictive metrics and analysis helping you to see problems before it's too late for corrective action

Campaign managers and the directors of the marketing functions benefit from a dashboard aimed a bit lower: the campaign scorecard. The scorecard is a more-granular version of the marketing dashboard, but specific to the campaign goals and objectives identified in the IMP.

Examples of campaign-level scorecard features include the following:

- Performance of the overall campaign against the primary campaign objectives

- Demonstration of how each program contributes to the campaign

- Performance of the key marketing activities and offers that support the campaign

- Pinpoint problem areas at a tactical level

- Budget overview at the campaign level

And finally, marketing leaders at every level (from the PR manager to the event coordinator to the CMO) need the ability to perform ad hoc reports on the most important marketing activities and offers. This type of fine-tuned reporting allows power users to overlap the marketing dashboard with the sales force automation system to drill down and get even more insight into lead trends and conversion rates. Activity reports need to be available daily or easily produced as needed.

Examples of custom reporting include the following:

- Source of qualified leads by media type

- Comparison of web downloads versus web hits

- Cost per advertising impression or press mention

- Any of a wide variety of other activity metrics

But again, managing metrics for metrics' sake is not productive. Attempting to manage a series of metrics for every activity is a waste of time with obvious diminishing returns. Instead, the team needs to focus on only those metrics that are most important because knowing that information will help the leaders make the best, most accurate real-time decisions possible. Above all else, the right metrics reporting tool needs to be created for the right internal audience.

Observational insight versus contextual insight

Key marketing metrics must be able to be captured quickly, even instantly. But not all metrics are mathematical in nature. In fact, there are two types of metrics that marketing leaders and campaign managers must always pay attention to.

Observational insights: managing the numbers

Contextual insight: understanding the reasons behind the numbers

Observational insights are what we've been mainly focused on so far. But contextual insights are equally important. It's not enough to know what the numbers are saying. We need to know the reasons why. Reasons may be linked to any of the following:

- **External context:** What trends are driving prospect behavior? These trends may be related to generational preferences (e.g., understanding how baby boomers versus echo generation prospects respond), time based (e.g., due to seasonality) or cultural (e.g., regional preferences), etc. To manage this analysis, many larger organizations have a market analyst or small analyst team just for this purpose.

- **Internal context:** How are the numbers being worked internally? Does your company have the right processes in place to digest the numbers? Are the marketers skilled enough to correctly analyze the meaning behind the numbers? Metrics training is an area many marketing teams are investing in. Workshops and seminars can help marketers better understand how to crunch the numbers and correctly interpret the results.

Critical success factors for managing the metrics management process

The world of marketing metrics is complex. Deciding what to measure for your business requires some careful thought because it is not always obvious. However, I can offer you three critical success factors that every world-class marketing organization must embrace to ensure success. Understanding these will help you build a solid framework that will help you optimize all of your marketing efforts.

1. Start at the top

Metrics definition and management must start at the top and work down. Measuring marketing metrics on individual activities out of context from the master campaign and the overall business objective is like trying to shut the barn door after the horse has gone. Metrics focused solely on the tactics will help the media managers (e.g., press relations manager, advertising manager) understand how well they have executed their activity, but it will not tell them if the activity was part of an optimal marketing mix. Nor will these individual metrics tell you if your marketing budget was well spent. To answer those loftier questions, metrics management must be embraced as part of the comprehensive campaign development process. The process starts with the CMO with daily involvement and oversight from the campaign manager.

2. Assign a metrics tsar

Metrics management and analysis is a critical task. Although everyone in marketing needs to be held accountable to a set of relevant, meaningful metrics, companies can benefit greatly by assigning at least one seasoned marketing analyst to oversee the metrics development, gathering, and presentation (i.e., creation of the dashboards) process. In fact, creation of the executive and campaign dashboards is a weighty assignment, especially the first time organizations tackle it. Having an assigned individual not only gives visible support of the metrics criteria, but it greatly speeds the time to execution of the dashboards and scorecards. Having said that, once the process and reporting tools are in place (and ultimately automated), a full time resource may not be required.

If your company is relying on the best intentions of the marketing team to manually capture any assortment of metrics, you are getting a poor return on their efforts. I recommend hiring an outside consultant or assigning an internal marketing leader for a quarter or two to assess your current metrics process and develop a custom set of dashboard and reporting templates.

3. Invest in metrics training and tools

Don't assume that every member of your marketing team understands the best metrics for their function or programs. Until recently, metrics management was treated like an unwanted stepchild nobody wanted to own. But gone are the days when a CMO could wave her hands and ignore the consequences of her decisions. Executive teams and company boards are demanding metrics be managed in a professional, visible way. Improving the skill level of every marketing employee is always a good investment. This is especially true in metrics management.

Look for marketing consultants and training organizations that can facilitate working sessions where teams can explore and debate which metrics to monitor, and which numbers to crunch. Through case studies and workshops, teams can learn how to critique their campaigns and discover the reasons behind the numbers. There are a growing number of very good marketing consultants and service providers who have made it their business to help marketing teams improve marketing operations and understand which metrics to use and when. In addition, a Google search will quickly identify a number of helpful online directories and resources on the topic. Here are a few to get you started:

Online resources:

- **Marketing Sherpa** (www.marketingsherpa.com) is a provider of practical marketing case studies and know-how

- **Marketing Profs** (www.marketingprofs.com) is a resource of marketing articles, case studies, marketing research

- **The GotoSiliconValley.com Business Directory**
  (www.gotosiliconvalley.com) is a resource directory for start-ups
  and entrepreneurs based in the San Francisco bay area.

Tools:

- Marketing automation packages such as Eloqua
  (www.eloqua.com), MarketBright (www.marketbright.com), and
  NetLine (www.netline.com)

- Marketing Performance Management solutions such as Cognos
  (www.cognos.com) and Hyperion (www.hyperion.com). (Hyperion
  was recently acquired by Oracle.)

7 The Role of the Campaign Manager

Nothing can hinder the success of a marketing campaign faster than an unseasoned campaign manager. So, what exactly is the role of the campaign manager and what is the profile of the most effective campaign managers? This chapter answers these questions and provides helpful tips that can accelerate the campaign development process, remove frustration, and produce better results.

"A leader is best when people barely know he exists, when his work is done, his aim fulfilled, they will say: we did it ourselves."[11]
Lao-Tzu, the father of Taoism

An often misunderstood role in business is that of the campaign manager. This nebulous position provokes reactions from peers that range from enthusiastic engagement to feared resentment. The difference depends on how the position of the campaign manager is first introduced to the team. But, it also depends heavily on the chemistry of the person who holds it.

---

11. Brainy Quote, http://tinyurl.com/2ra2rd.

The effective execution of this role can dramatically improve the results of any marketing campaign or new product launch. With so much at stake, why then do so many campaign managers fail? I worked as a campaign manager and then as a director of campaign management for eight years at HP, Sun, and Ariba. Today I coach campaign managers throughout the hi-tech industry. Here are just a few of the lessons I've learned about successful campaign managers.

What is a campaign manager, really?

If designing a marketing campaign were equated to building a house, the campaign manager would be the architect. The team members are the contractors with specific areas of strategic and tactical expertise.

The campaign manager brings strategic insight, tactical coordination, and leadership to driving a cross-functional team towards its goal. The best campaign managers are part customer advocate, part product evangelist, and part professional facilitator. They are not engineering or content experts, per se (Plenty of those experts can be found within their team). A brief description of a campaign manager can be found in Figure 35.

The campaign manager is most often a senior individual contributor reporting to a CMO or senior VP. Although, in some contexts, they may be part of a product marketing or business unit team. (However, in the latter structure extra care must be taken to avoid organizational conflicts of interest.) Campaign managers typically have no direct reports but work cross-functionally to influence a wide variety of marketing functions and regional teams as well as executive management. Employees unfamiliar with matrix management models may find this a difficult model to understand at first. But, with practice, the value-add of this leadership role becomes clear to everyone. The campaign manager oversees and coordinates the development and final approval of the marketing campaign strategy and owns the process for the creation of the IMP.

Definition of the Campaign Manager

- The general manager of the entire IMP process
- The author of the final IMP
- Moderator & facilitator of key meetings:
  - Kickoff
  - Synchronization meetings
  - Program development brainstorming sessions
- The lead presenter in steering committee review meetings
- An escalation path to help team members identify issues and confirm priorities
- (*In the execution phase*) The leader who calls periodic meetings to assess progress and measure/analyze results and drive real-time changes to the campaign

But the campaign manager does not . . .

- Dictate specific tactics or actions arbitrarily or unilaterally
- Micro-manage the details and tactics

Figure 35: Definition of a Campaign Manager

When do you need a campaign manager?

As we introduced in Chapter 2, not all companies may need a formal campaign manager role. But, if yours is a growing company with a complex sales and marketing model, you should consider adding the campaign manager role within your team. Some considerations that a campaign manager may be appropriate for your business include the following internal and external indicators. The campaign manager is the perfect leader to guide the team through these dimensions of complexity. This role is instrumental in architecting successful marketing strategies that will maximize your company's marketing investment.

Internal Indicators

- There is a clear lack of coordination between marketing, sales, and the business units.

- Management is unsatisfied and frustrated with marketing's contributions, but they are unsure where the problems lie.

- There is disagreement between sales and marketing regarding how many leads are actually being produced.

- The business plan calls for the execution of high-stakes campaigns such as a company repositioning effort or new product introductions.

External Indicators

- Past marketing programs failed to produce the required results, and you're not sure why.

- Yours is a complex selling process. The sales cycle is 9–12 months or longer, with multiple people involved in the decision-making process.

- Customers and prospects have exhibited confusion regarding your messaging.

- Your competitors are stealing market share away from you.

- Your business is evolving from a direct sales model to a channel-focused model. As a result, the marketing campaigns need to be reformulated for the channel.

Five success factors of effective campaign managers

So, what separates great campaign managers from the rest of us? I've had the privilege to work with some of the best campaign managers in hi-tech companies anywhere. I've also seen first-hand the trauma brought about by inexperienced people who didn't know what they were doing. Figure 36 shares a few of the characteristics found in every one of the best campaign managers I've known.

Characteristics of Effective Campaign Managers

- A recognized, well-rounded marketing leader familiar with the target market
- Proven leadership in "managing by objective"
- Attentive to detail, but doesn't micro-manage
- Diplomatic and politically savvy
- Patient
- A good facilitator, seasoned in active listening techniques
- Excellent written and oral communicator
  - With the team
  - Upper management
  - Steering committee
- Knows when and how to provide constructive feedback in real time during public meetings; knows when and how to provide direct feedback in one-on-one settings
- Is prepared to make hard decisions and trade-offs for the greater good of the campaign
- Most of all, doesn't let their ego get in the way of sound decision-making

---

Figure 36: The Most Effective Campaign Managers Have These Traits in Common

Campaign development teams may have as many as 50 individuals or as few as five. Team members may include employees, contractors, and consultants. Because of the diversity of the team, the campaign manager must be comfortable, in fact thrive, on the ambiguity that may exist regarding roles and responsibilities. It all boils down to the five key skills of effective campaign managers. The best campaign managers have them; a lack of any one of these can doom any campaign.

1. **They are experienced all-around marketing athletes with proven leadership abilities.** Clearly, the best campaign managers understand how marketing works: they are not engineers who are breaking into marketing for the first time. They don't need to know everything about every marketing angle, but they have deep marketing knowledge in at least one of the following areas: customers and target markets, marketing strategy creation, product knowledge, marketing expertise in a specific region, proven leadership in a marketing media type (such as field marketing or press relations). In addition, the best campaign managers are senior individual contributors coming from being a senior manager or director in another marketing function. Thus, they bring marketing knowledge and political savvy to the role.

2. **They know when and how to delegate.** A campaign manager takes her success not from her own actions, but from the accomplishments of the team. As seen in the Lao Tsu quote at the beginning go this chapter, effective campaign managers remember to say "we" not "I." As such, delegation is the campaign manager's most effective tool. Good campaign managers know a little about a lot of things, but they don't know everything. Whereas some inexperienced campaign managers may feel threatened by this, the best campaign managers do not. They are not afraid to let others lead. They look for opportunities to involve others in mapping the campaign strategy. In so doing, they encourage and nurture the team's passion and energy.

3. **They are excellent in "managing upwards" and gaining and maintaining visibility for the team.** Every business has its political nuances. The best campaign managers can spot these and keep the team out of trouble, while interfacing with management proactively and effectively. Team players look to

campaign managers to resolve or escalate issues when required. Campaign managers are adept at managing the process so that the team players can do what they do best.

4. **They are accountable, but they don't micromanage.** This is a tricky balance because campaign managers are responsible for delivering the campaign strategy and plan, but they can't build it alone. Their ultimate success is achieved by being a resource and guide for the team and ensuring that their collective contributions are aligned appropriately.

   When campaign managers cross the line and micromanage the deliverables, team members may take offense and sabotage the process. To avoid this trap, the best campaign managers add value, not by dictating action, but by setting clear objectives and timelines and working to remove obstacles. They always focus on the "big picture", lead the charge, and then get out the way.

5. **They know when to disband the team.** When the IMP has been created and approved, the job of the campaign development team is over, and the role of the campaign manager changes. Once Gate 2 approval has been reached, the campaign manager's immediate duty is to celebrate the team's achievement, thanking them for their time, energy, and accomplishments.

   Visible recognition is always appreciated by team members and important for morale. The marketing media managers will now transition to executing the programs. They are perfectly capable of doing so within the operating parameters of their own functions; a campaign manager acting like a clucking mother hen is unwelcome and unneeded. Now, the campaign manager's role shifts to focus on results and reporting back to the steering committee with status updates and recommendations for campaign adjustments should market or business conditions change.

Executive endorsement

There can be no question that executive endorsement is critical to success. In fact, without active, visible executive support, the campaign manager will flounder and the team members will not be inclined to break out of their siloed behavior. Sometimes the introduction of the campaign manager role may feel to some like a punitive act. In no way is the addition of this new role meant as a slight against any part of the marketing organization. On the contrary, this role is intended to be a guiding resource to ensure that all marketers have the information and leadership support they need to perform at their best and deliver the maximum marketing ROI.

Campaign management case studies

Sometimes it's helpful to see where and when companies decided to adopt the role of the campaign manager. Here are a few of my own experiences.

Defragmentation

In the late '90s, the worldwide customer support organization of a large computer company was approaching $4 billion in annual revenue. Four divisions comprised this business unit, each with its own product marketing staff and its own business agenda. Corporate marketing was a centralized resource supporting these divisions. Unfortunately, conflict was common between the divisions as they fought to control the limited corporate marketing resources and budget. The result was fragmented marketing messages and tension between the teams. It was even worse when it became clear that those projects that were getting done were not necessarily the projects that were most needed. Instead, the resources were being allocated to those product marketing managers who "yelled the loudest." Obviously, this was not the most effective approach to prioritization and decision making.

To alleviate this frustration, they created a new team of senior marketing campaign managers that reported directly to the group marcom manager. Although managed centrally, a campaign manager was assigned to each division. This team of campaign managers worked with their peers in corporate marketing and their divisional counterparts to architect a new campaign development process that centered around the customer, not the product. Their collective efforts put a stop to the creation of an unending stream of fragmented marketing activities. Instead of literally hundreds of individual marketing projects managed independently, six integrated campaigns were created.

These campaigns were structured to address the divisions' business priorities while being respectful of the customer at the same time. These core campaigns were developed in conjunction with the annual budgeting process, then updated quarterly. Improved teamwork and alignment between the divisions resulted in more consistent messaging created with less frustration, and the execution of cleverer marketing campaigns with greater international leverage. After a year of developing and proving the value of this new function, the campaign management team became one of the most respected and sought after teams within the company's marketing community.

Acquisition Integration

A large software security company had grown through a series of acquisitions. Its marketing department had blossomed to more than 700 individuals spread out across the world. However, each acquisition had its own way of marketing; and, these ways continued to be practiced by the employees who had brought them. This lack of consistency created some obvious problems for the worldwide marketing team. What was needed was a way to unite the global team with a common process that would prioritize market opportunities and reveal synergies and gaps.

After a careful assessment of their internal marketing operations process, the CMO and her marketing staff set forth to build a new campaign development process built on industry best practices. The CMO set the agenda for change with passion and excitement. An anointed marketing operations team led the charge to drive the mechanics, complete with the formation of an operations oversight committee and an executive steering committee. The campaign management role was created to oversee the creation of IMPs for their five global campaigns. The team used an assortment of best-of-breed templates and techniques to rally their international teams to focus and set priorities that are continuing to drive higher levels of marketing ROI for their global efforts.

Just for campaign managers . . .

If you are a campaign manager, or you are managing a team of campaign managers, pay close attention! This section summarizes some of the most important tips and tricks I've learned. I pass them on in the hope that they will help you avoid some of the most common mistakes, while accelerating you on your path to success.

Secrets for working cross-organizationally

- Invite input and feedback at every stage of your IMP development process.

- Practice active listening techniques.

- Invite regional participation at the kickoff meeting, but don't expect full involvement to begin until the synchronization meetings. Rely on global marketing colleagues to reach out to regions in parallel.

- Budgeting issues will arise. Build a budget-leadership team (of 2-3 senior directors/managers where possible) within the larger campaign team to help you define and resolve budget barriers.

- Escalate to the steering committee only after other avenues have failed.

- Build a forum just for campaign managers where you can share your own insights and best practices on a routine basis. Look for ways to build and encourage synergy between campaigns when appropriate.

- Over-communicate the objective, strategy, and status of your campaign to others in marketing in both formal and informal ways. Just because you share this information once doesn't mean everyone knows or understands it.

Recognizing success

Sometimes seeing the value in the campaign development process is illusive because it is intangible. This doesn't mean that the process isn't working. It just may mean you haven't looked in the right places. Success looks like:

* Team members working cross-organizationally on their own (i.e. in meetings not called by the campaign manager) in support of campaign objectives

* Productive and constructive "what if" scenarios that spark creativity

* Structured, but flexible, synchronization meeting agendas with lots of engagement and discussion

* The development of highly creative, interactive programs that involve multiple functions that meet the campaign objectives

* Consistent use of product positioning, messages, and campaign terminology (e.g., campaign, programs, activities, offers)

* All team members "singing off of the same song sheet"

* Positive feedback from the business units, divisions, general management, sales team that marketing is having an improved, noticeable impact on the sales cycle

* High marketing morale with engaged team members

Final thoughts for campaign managers

The campaign manager position is of critical importance to the success of the integrated marketing campaigns. However, if you are a campaign manager don't let this go to your head. Success is NOT just about you.

Be mindful of the following:

* How your campaign fits within the strategic planning process

* How your campaign plays in the regional planning process

- Other campaigns (don't outflank other campaign managers)

- Making good business decisions

You've achieved a unique role in your organization that will expand your leadership, management, and creativity skills. Have fun and grow with it. To help you on your way, here are a few of the most often referred to books in my personal library. I don't believe the content of these will ever go out of style.

Additional resources

- *Getting to Yes – Negotiating Agreement Without Giving In,* Roger Fisher and William Ury
  http://tinyurl.com/35gc94

- *How to Win Friends & Influence People*, Dale Carnegie
  http://tinyurl.com/38c6kw

- *All I Really Need to Know I Learned in Kindergarten*, Robert Fulghum
  http://tinyurl.com/2ns3j6

- *Positioning: The Battle for Your Mind,* Al Ries and Jack Trout
  http://tinyurl.com/2wfjlo

8 Overcoming Objections

Here we explore the top nine objections all teams face when rolling out a campaign development process. For each obstacle, we offer a practical approach to remove the obstacle and improve team productivity.

"Stand up to your obstacles and do something about them. You will find that they haven't half the strength you think they have."[12]
Norman Vincent Peale, author of "The Power of Positive Thinking"

Embarking on the campaign development process to produce world-class IMPs is not easy. It takes effort and requires changes to internal processes, planning templates, and even skill levels of the marketing staff. But, the rewards are genuine and the opportunity to create even higher levels of customer loyalty are achievable by nurturing an intelligent and respectful relationship with your target audiences. But change is often difficult for people and organizations. Here are nine of the most

---

12. Brainy Quote, http://tinyurl.com/n3rj6.

common objections and how marketing leaders at every level can maneuver around them to expedite the path to marketing success.

1) Now is not a good time. We are too busy to start a new campaign development process.

In today's global marketplace there is no shortage of work that must be done. Everyone has (or should have) goals and objectives that drive their day-to-day work. However, many companies (both Fortune 500 companies as well as start-ups) find themselves executing a variety of marketing projects that aren't really part of an overall defined marketing plan. In other words, they are busy writing press releases, generating emails, coordinating webinars, but none of these activities are linked to each other – at least not to full extent they should be. If you find yourself in this predicament, but with executive or time pressures that prevent you from adopting a new process, what can you do?

Luckily for us, the science and art of campaign development is not an "all or nothing" game. In fact, for most companies it is not practical to throw out existing processes and start over. Instead, the answer is to look for opportunities to make small but meaningful improvements over time. Process improvement may start in requiring all marketing members to embrace a consistent value proposition format (see Chapter 3 and Appendix A), or in adopting or fine-tuning your IMP template (see Chapters 4 and Appendix B), or in organizing a sales-and-marketing team workshop around creating program blueprints (see Chapter 5 and Appendix C). The point is to find one obvious thing that needs improvement and provide enough guidance and direction to make improvements on it quickly. This is your first step in working the larger process. Taking positive action, no matter how small, is usually much better than taking no action. Chapter 9 provides some additional perspective to help you take the first step.

2) Sales people are a challenge to deal with. It's too much trouble to coordinate with them.

When marketing teams act independently from sales, the results will always be less than optimal. There is an almost unlimited number of ways for marketing to be busy. The key question is, what activities should marketing be executing (and when) that will help the sales team close more deals more quickly?

The marketing-sales alignment should be a topic of every day discussion, not just once a year. By that I mean that developing a joint sales and marketing strategy at the beginning of the year and then discussing feedback in real time and making course corrections should be a standard operating procedure for all companies. Some companies will leave this interaction to the discretion of each individual; however, world-class marketing organizations drive and encourage this process by setting up a series of marketing-sales touch points to review progress quarterly, if not monthly. In short, marketing and sales teams should be working with a "hand in glove" expectation and mentality.

As an example, many companies hold quarterly marketing-sales summits. These ½ day to full day meetings are typically led by the CMO, but include representatives from corporate and regional marketing and sales teams. These are interactive meetings designed to create tighter bonds between the teams while solving business issues in real time. If the sales-marketing relationship has been strained in the past, consider hiring an outside business-savvy facilitator to guide your summit. They can ease tension and make the meeting productive. But, not all facilitators are alike. Look for one who is technology savvy and understands your business.

3) We've got a backlog of marketing tactics in play. Restrategizing them just isn't practical.

You're right. And, unless we are building a new company from the ground up, there will always be a backlog of tactics that must be executed. The key to success is in recognizing and separating what can be changed from what shouldn't be changed. For example, it may be largely impractical to halt any marketing tactics that are currently underway. If the strategy for the direct marketing activity has already been signed-off and the creative team is already busy writing, then we probably want to let that activity run its course. However, the question is, "What should happen next?"

Planning is a future-focused activity. Don't worry about justifying current or past activities into a not-yet-completed plan. There is little value in that. Instead, set a time horizon in the future against which new campaigns will be set. For example, a CMO might state, "All new campaigns that will be executed next fiscal year will follow the new campaign development process." That simple statement allows for a buffer zone for the marketing team to get today's work done while allowing them time to adjust their schedules to prepare for planning.

4) Planning is largely irrelevant because we must be open to all revenue opportunities. We really can't say "no" when sales asks us to do something for them.

This objection is probably the toughest for marketing teams to wrestle with because there can be some painful political fallout by saying "no," especially when a request for a new marketing project is tied to a potential sale. Regardless, the most effective marketing teams are those that have the courage to drive focus by helping the executive and sales teams agree upon which target markets and which opportunities are the most important. We all know that trying to be all things to all markets always leads to sub-standard results and confused customers and prospects. Bottom line: You can only say "no" with confidence when you can explain what you are already saying "yes" to and why that's a higher priority.

There is a common misconception about addressing this objection, however. Many people confuse being "marketing driven" with being "market driven." So, let me be clear: we are talking about the market conditions and expectations driving our decision process. We are not talking about the marketing team arbitrarily dictating a course of action. When a company becomes market driven, it is really deciding where, when, and how its proactive marketing investment and activities should be executed. It is not saying that it won't accept a sale from some other non-target customer.

But, because we always have limited resources, unplanned opportunities will arise and there will be cases where campaigns, programs, and activities will need to be further prioritized. To help alleviate internal conflict and provide a venue for productive debate and decision-making, world-class companies look to guidance from their cross-functional steering committee to evaluate new sales opportunities that may require a shift in direction from the campaign strategy. The steering committee, when used properly, can be a very effective tool and guide for escalating important issues that have a direct impact on the vision and mission of the company and the marketing team's ability to successful execute.

5) These planning processes are great for corporate, but they are not helpful for managing regional activities. We need to do our own thing.

There is a lot of truth in this objection. The regions and the countries are all unique with markets and languages that require special attention. Distance from the US offices makes real-time communication challenging, especially when teams want to set up a world-wide conference call that involve team members from Europe as well as Asia. But world-class marketing organizations have found a way to work the process and harness the power of strategic thinking so that regional campaigns can be executed more quickly and cost less. Here are a few tips:

- To engage regional support early, take time to explain what's in it for them. Their participation will allow them to better leverage messaging and positioning, marketing funds, tools and templates. This will help them speed regional execution.

- The entire regional team does not need to participate in every part of the campaign development process. Instead, look for a single knowledgeable resource that can best represent the needs of the region. This resource will be critical in helping the team to think beyond US borders.

- In addition to a worldwide campaign team, establish an EMEA sub-team, an Asia Pacific sub-team, and a Japan sub-team. Ask for the regional team leader to work with their local teams to create recommendations that can feed into the broader process. This encourages wider participation, and ultimately improves the likelihood of regional adoption of the plan once complete.

- Alter the times of team meetings, within reason, to make it more convenient for regional representatives to participate. Although the headquarters team will complain about having to work late in order to participate on a call with Japan, it's only fair that the time zone challenges be shared at least once in a while.

- Setting proper expectations with all team members regarding how the campaign will be adapted to each region is vital. The goals of the campaign should be consistent and clear across regions. However, it is likely that the tactics used to achieve the objectives will differ. This is expected and makes sense. For example, the use of faxes may not work as a delivery mechanism in Germany, but they may be preferred in Australia. Don't let team members get upset if they see differences in the deployment of tactics. It really doesn't matter as long as the team is managing activities to achieve the central objective above all else.

6) Changing our campaign development process is too hard.

Overcoming resistance to change is one of the toughest objections to overcome because it means that team members must change their behaviors and expectations. For this new process to succeed, there are a number of needed critical factors. For rapid success, here are the first three that will set the framework for a productive engagement model.

1. The need for change must be visibly and actively communicated from the CEO and CMO. Adoption and adherence to the campaign development process must be advocated from the executive staff. Only executive management can communicate

with authority the need and urgency for embracing the campaign development process. This is why visible senior management commitment to the campaign at the earliest stage is so critical.

2. Set expectations for involvement in the new process and include these expectations as part of everyone's individual performance evaluations. Directives without expectations and measures are just words. People need to know that actions and results will be tracked and rewarded, as appropriate. And rewards should be celebrated and shared for individual performance as well as for team performance.

3. Lay out a clear time-table against which this planning process will unfold. Even though the details are likely still undecided, the backdrop for the process needs to be established and communicated.

Ultimately the choice is between doing what is easy and what is most effective. Keep in mind that your competitors have already embraced many of these practices. What are you waiting for?

7) The integrated marketing plan (IMP) will only sit on a shelf and gather dust.

We've all probably experienced the frustration of having to create large tomes that go unread. When this happens, it is usually the fault of the management team not being serious or committed to the process and the value it provides. How can we best keep the spirit and intent of the IMP alive?

Executive management's visible commitment to the process is the first step. But we also need to be sure that the IMP doesn't just sit on the shelf. Once the IMP has been approved at Gate 2, the campaign manager's duty is to be the steward for the campaign, keeping the spirit of the campaign alive. The campaign manager will track results and monitor the market's reaction, as markets are dynamic and ever changing. If changes to the campaign are required, either because business or competitive conditions have changed, the campaign manager will reform her team to address the changes and update or amend the IMP.

8) There's too much confusion between the business units and marcom. No one knows who is driving the process.

The question is really, which organization controls the campaign managers? If campaign managers report to marcom, does marcom control all the cards? If campaign management reports to the business unit, does the business unit trump marcom? This objection is very serious and indicates the complexity of many Fortune 500 organizational structures. Whose side is the campaign manager on? The answer, of course, is that the campaign manager should always be on the customer's side!

Ideally, the campaign managers are part of a marketing operations team that reports directly to the CMO. This is ideal because the campaign manager can remain unbiased as they are not directly tied to any specific product or marketing group. They can approach the campaign from the customer's perspective and be their advocate through the development process. However, marketing operations teams are a relatively new trend in marketing; not all companies have them yet. As such, the ownership for crafting integrated marketing plans may reside in marcom, product marketing teams, or elsewhere within cross-functional business units.

The good news is that this process and function can exist in any structure as long as the business and campaign objectives are clearly established and reflected in the campaign management charter and each campaign manager's personal goals. Regardless of the organizational structure, the campaign development process and the criteria for campaign prioritization and decision making must be documented and communicated broadly so expectations can be set properly. More so, this information must be communicated consistently and constantly reinforced by each of the marketing leaders of the different organizations. Ultimately, this is the only way the confusion will evaporate.

9) I can't plan unless I know how much money I have to spend.

This objection is a favorite of marcom managers everywhere. But here is the fallacy: reality tells us that we will never have as much money and time as we would like. So waiting for a politicized committee to give us a number before we can make a recommendation damages the credibility of the marketing team. Instead, we need to turn this situation around and lead the budget discussion, not be subservient to it.

Our best value comes when we can guide the executive budgeting process by providing an order-of-magnitude budget estimate required for achieving a specific campaign objective. This is where marketing teams can exercise leadership in addition to being expert tacticians. What budget is required to achieve the campaign objective? Can we meet the objective with the budget we have? How much of the campaign objective is at risk if our budget is limited? What are the trade offs? These are the budget-related questions that campaigns teams need to wrestle with.

Having said that, we all know that budgeting is a complex give-and-take process that spans several months. As such a campaign team must be nimble to scale up or down their recommendation to match the available budget. Here are a few tips for building a reasonable budget estimate:

- **The art of budgeting is about making trade-offs.** The three variables marketers have to work with are scope, schedule, and cost. Reality tells us that when you lock down two dimensions, the third will align itself accordingly. As the saying goes, "You want it fast, good, and cheap? Pick two." If you are fortunate to have been given a clear budget, focus your time in determining what you can do to maximize results within that budget. If the scope or schedule are the pre-defined factors, then the required budget will be determined by the choice of required activities and offers to achieve the business or market objective.

- **Take a look at history.** Look at what your marketing team spent last year to gain a basis for the order of magnitude for your likely marketing budget. Even if your marketing team didn't produce an IMP, the total dollars available to you will probably be in the same ball park.

- **Look at industry best practices.** Many marketing consultants and vendors can give you data for producing a budget with confidence. Look for a consultant/vendor who you trust. Share with them the exercise you are going through and ask for their help in estimating costs and timing, based on real projects they have managed.

- **Check with the American Marketing Association and other marketing trades.** They have access to experts throughout the industry who have written articles and books on a variety of subjects. Ask them to provide you with an introduction to a resource or two for you off whom you can bounce budgeting ideas.

- **Search the Internet.** As with the personal relationships you can gain through marketing associations, you can also gain access to an overwhelming amount of information on the Web. Focus your search criteria and keep to the authors who have written multiple articles or books on the subject of budgeting. That way, you'll avoid the ramblings of unqualified bloggers.

9 Taking the First Step

So, what does it take to apply this best practice approach to your business today? It is not as hard as you might think to make meaningful improvements immediately. This chapter tells you how to get started.

"Marketing is not an event, but a process . . . It has a beginning, a middle, but never an end, for it is a process. You improve it, perfect it, change it, even pause it. But you never stop it completely." [13]
Jay Conrad Levinson, noted author of the Guerilla marketing books

Getting started

The most difficult step in any journey is the first one: the personal decision to invest time and effort into bettering your campaign development process. Once you've made the personal commitment, where is the best place to start? The answer is, it depends.

---

13. Museum Marketing Tips, http://tinyurl.com/2na725.

Step 1: Focus on three things

Fortunately for us, crafting a world-class campaign development process is not a zero-sum game. In other words, it's not about throwing out what you have in favor of reinventing the total process. In most cases (unless you are building a new business from scratch), that approach is unrealistic.

Success can be achieved with small, but important and impactful, changes made over time. So, instead of being instantly overwhelmed by the 100 differences between your reality and the process described in this book, perform a quick assessment of your process to determine the first three elements of your process where improvement is needed. What are the three most important things that need to be addressed? Focus on those, and don't be distracted by anything else (for now).

These process elements may be the application of a consistent IMP template, adoption of consistent terminology (campaign, program, activity, offer), or establishing a steering committee to help with escalations. I have no doubt that you already know a couple of areas where you'd like to see your team and your process improve. As the change agent for the marketing team and your business, you decide what initial steps need to be taken.

Regardless of your role in the marketing organization, if you can apply any of the lessons of this book to three small areas of your own process, then this book will have provided its value. Focusing on three improvement areas gives your team a chance to experience a tangible success. Each success, however small, will help you reinforce the commitment to the larger goal of creating a world-class integrated marketing process that is fun, engaging, and differentiating.

Step 2: Perform a campaign development assessment

If you are the CMO or leader of your marketing organization, the next step is up to you. Each marketing organization is unique in the details of how it functions, how it interacts with sales, and the skills of its team members. Before you can understand what changes are needed for optimum, long-term success, you need to conduct a marketing assessment.

"But assessments cost too much and I don't need one because I know what I need to do," I hear you say. Let's be realistic: your boss is holding your feet to the fire to deliver marketing results. You don't have the time or bandwidth to personally dig into the details and really understand where the improvements in planning, processes, or people are needed. The good news is that you can benefit greatly by involving others (either team members or outside experts) to help you conduct an assessment. The good news is also that a marketing assessment need not take a long time or cost much money. In fact, most audits can be completed in under a week or two and conclude with a set of action-oriented recommendations. It is well worth the investment and will save you from surprises down the road.

What's covered in a typical campaign development assessment?

An assessment will give you a pragmatic view of your outbound marketing communications ecosystem and will help you understand whether improvements are required related to the planning templates, operational processes, or people skills. Knowing where the gaps are will help you identify where mid-term to long-term success lies.

1. **Planning:** Your ability to effectively plan marketing campaigns and programs.

2. **Processes:** A hard look at the methods and tasks used to create, gain approval, execute, and analyze results of each marketing campaign.

3. **People:** An assessment of the skill sets residing in your staff and their abilities.

But you don't need to spend money on an assessment yet. The best place to start is with your own self assessment. Grade your organization's effectiveness in each quadrant shown in Table 1. How would you assess the health of your organization along these dimensions?

Table 1: Grade Your Organization in This Self-assessment Grid

	"Voice of the Customer" Intelligence Gathering	Outbound Marketing Communications
Planning Templates and Tools		
Processes		
People Skills		

Techniques to help you hear the "voice of the customer"

Every successful campaign starts with a solid understanding of the customer.

How well do you understand the issues driving your customers' businesses? Does the marketing communications team have access to this information? Do they share a common understanding of the business drivers and challenges your customers face? Once this information is collected, do you have a process for systematically making this information available and accessible to the rest of the marketing staff?

The marketing assessor will interview a variety of staff members to identify the current level of available market intelligence. They can determine what, if any, statistically rigorous market research exists on the interests, needs, perceptions, opinions, and expectations of your customers, prospects, and other supporters or stakeholders. Information may be gathered from customer visits, product focus groups, customer advisory boards, sales reps, analyst interviews, etc. The assessor will also take a look at how your company houses and shares this information. This repository can be your greatest asset — or your worst albatross. Most of the time, this information is captured in only a few marketers' heads or their hard drives. Without a repository, you are at risk of losing this valuable corporate information when they leave the company.

How successful are your outbound marketing communications today?

Are you executing multi-faceted integrated programs that encourage your prospects and customers to engage in an ongoing dialog? Or, are you executing a series of isolated, disconnected marketing activities? Do you have seasoned marketing leaders building a thoughtful campaign, or do you have well-intentioned tacticians pulling triggers without thought? What grade will you give your organization?

Your marketing programs should be strategic, targeted, and cost-effective with objectives and metrics based on industry response standards and your organization's historic response rates. Feedback from your customers can help you determine the communication channels of most interest to specific target segments. A marketing assessor can help you fine-tune your campaign development process, ensuring that it ties in with your key business planning processes and timeline. They can also determine if you are utilizing the most effective range of promotional channels and tactics, while not relying too heavily on just one or two formats, such as email or events. They can also help you assess the skills of your marketing staff with a range of ideas and recommendations for building better, stronger marketers.

Step 3: Make it visible

Whatever steps you decide to take, make them visible. Improving the campaign development process is a very important, pragmatic undertaking. Success requires that the drive behind these improvements be voiced and echoed from the CEO down to the individual contributors. And, I'm not just talking about producing dashboards and scorecards. I'm talking about the CMO, in hallway conversations, personally endorsing the contributions made by team members who are actively supporting the process; the CEO rallying employees in quarterly meetings; and employees at every level sharing real-time results and encouraging each other. Here are just a few best practices I've witnessed CMOs and campaign leaders use to rally their troops:

- Once you identify your three areas for improvement (step 1), involve team members. Invite, encourage, and require participation.

- Start a new tradition of quarterly marketing-sales summits to review priorities and compare campaign results with the sales pipeline. Tell executive management and the sales organization about your long-term goal of improving the campaign development process. Share your expectations with them.

- Once implemented, don't let go. And when you've implemented each milestone, acknowledge each success. Watch for results. Even small improvements, tangible or intangible benefits, are noteworthy.

Five rules for marketing leaders

As the CMO, marketing leader, or campaign manager consider yourself a Michelangelo. Your campaign development process is your Sistine Chapel. Will your marketing campaigns tomorrow be copies of what you've done in the past, producing random results? Or will they be carefully crafted, engaging your target audience on their terms, becoming the basis for a long-term relationship with you? In closing, here are my five important rules for marketing leaders to live by:

Rule 1: The process of developing a winning marketing campaign is a marathon, not a sprint.

Good campaigns don't just happen. It takes time to architect an integrated, multi-faceted marketing campaign focused on achieving specific goals. The process needs to take into account marketing objectives, the prioritization of programs, and budget implications. Because of this complexity, the development and approval of a well-thought-out IMP can easily take 10–12 weeks. (At first glance, you may think this is ridiculously long. It is not. Remember the Sun example in Chapter 1. And consider that many marketing teams invest much longer than this to clean up lackluster marketing programs that were ill-planned and never produce meaningful results.) Be patient. Plan accordingly.

Rule 2: Integrated campaigns are built by cross-functional teams, not an isolated campaign manager.

A good campaign manager drives the process, but does not dictate the plan. Instead, the best campaign managers invite participation from regional and functional experts. They facilitate a process whereby the best, most effective plan will emerge.

Rule 3: "Ready, aim, fire." Set the strategy before executing tactics.

As mentioned earlier, campaign managers and their extended teams must avoid the temptation to produce "marketing popcorn." Like in playing a good game of chess, world-class marketers take the time to consider each next move before executing it. The strategy guides the tactics, not vice versa.

Rule 4: Use an outside, experienced marketing operations consultant to help develop and fine tune the campaign management process that fits your business.

You and your marketing staff are incredibly busy. When you are heads-down in working the process, it is often difficult to separate the symptoms from the root cause in process inefficiencies. This is where a seasoned marketing operations expert can help. Companies like HP, Informatica, Symantec, and others have invested in a trusted, unbiased outside resource to help them assess the effectiveness of their campaign development process and recommend specific actions for immediate improvement. The best marketing operations consultants are practical, pragmatic, and politically savvy. Partnering with them can help you accelerate the campaign development process while removing barriers and easing frustrations. If you are interested in making progress quickly, there is no better way to start.

Rule 5: Track results and make real-time course corrections.

Once the IMP is completed and approved, the team transitions into execution-mode. However, the campaign manager will continue to monitor results. The IMP is static in nature; but markets are dynamic. Thus, the most effective campaign managers set up mechanisms for tracking progress, communicating results often, and making course corrections in real-time in order to continually optimize the marketing mix.

As Jay Levinson states in his quote at the beginning of this chapter, the campaign development and management process is never ending. Marketing leaders at every level are constantly challenged to improving themselves and their processes in order to create a brand that is truly differentiating. You hold the keys to creating a new age of customer interaction that will separate you from your competition. The old rules of mass marketing and niche marketing no longer apply. It's about one-on-one person-to-person marketing that will make the difference.

People's expectations about how they are communicated with have changed and will continue to change. The campaign development process laid out in this book is your guide to embracing this challenge. Also, the templates for value propositions, IMP templates, and the seven program blueprints are included in the Appendices and available online at www.kickstartall.com/campaign_development.html. Take advantage of them.

In conclusion

The science and art of campaign development is not rocket science. There is probably nothing in this book which you did not already know at some level of your experience. What I have tried to do is to organize common sense and common experience in a way that provides a usable framework for thinking and acting. The more consistent these ideas are with your knowledge and intuition, the better. As with human nature, we all learn by doing. It is my sincere hope that this book will point you in a promising direction by making you aware of these ideas and how you can kickstart your marketing team to the "next level."

Good luck!

Appendices

For your easy reference the templates shown here are also available online at:

www.kickstartall.com/campaign_development.html

To access them, please register and use "**chessmaster**" as your password.

A. Value proposition template and example
B. Integrated Marketing Plan (IMP) template
C. The seven program blueprints

A Value Proposition Template

As we introduced in Chapter 3, six ingredients go into the construction of a solid value proposition: customer sets, value drivers, competitive positioning, evidence, internal views, and external views.

In the formation of a value proposition, a lot of data will be collected and analyzed. The value proposition template is designed to summarize this data in a way that tells a story about the unique value your company or product or solution delivers. Keep in mind that the value proposition, as we have illustrated in this template, is designed for internal audiences only. It is not the actual message to the customer or prospect. This is one of the single best tools you can use to ensure that everyone on your team understands the value you provide and how it relates to your target audiences.

The following is an example of a value proposition based on a real product: "Product X". The names of the company and their product have been omitted for confidentiality. This example provides insight into each piece of the value proposition equation, and then summarizes it in the template. (See Figure 37.)

Customer Set

Our target audience is CIOs of multinational companies in the financial services, hospitality, and manufacturing industries. These companies are the leaders in their industry and are forecasted to grow at twice the market rate over the next five years. These CIOs need the ability to quickly add IT capacity, anywhere in the world, at a moment's notice.

Problem/Need

A growing number of organizations need more IT capacity to meet current needs or take advantage of new opportunities, yet lack the space, power, time and money to add it to their existing data centers or build new ones using traditional approaches. These organizations are looking for a creative way to add IT capacity to meet their business needs without breaking the budget.

Value Driver

Product X is the world's first virtualized datacenter. Housed in a standard 20-foot shipping container, Product X can be deployed anywhere in the world within a matter of weeks – 1/10th the time it takes to deploy a traditional datacenter – at a fraction of the initial cost, with 3x the number of systems in equivalent space and with 20% more efficient cooling/power. Product X features shock absorption for easy transport and integrated and centralized state-of-the-art cooling, networking, and power distribution that optimize energy, space, and performance efficiency.

Competitive Positioning

Unlike custom datacenter-in-a-box solutions offered by Company Y created for disaster relief and military operations, our Product X is the world's first modular datacenter that is available for broad commercial use. In addition, our decision to house the solution in a standard 20-foot shipping container is novel. Shipping containers are designed to move goods anywhere in the world with maximum efficiency. Thus, it can be deployed anywhere there is electricity, chilled water, and an Internet connection – from the parking lot to an offshore oil rig.

Evidence

Early Product X deployments have demonstrated capacity for more than 500 CPUs, 2,000 cores or 8,000 compute threads. In addition, ROI studies conducted for Customers A, B, and C show customers saving as much as $350,000 in energy costs by locating a Product X datacenter near cheaper, renewable energy sources. Industry analysts P and Q have produced new reports showing the business and operational benefits of complementing IT environments with this unique approach.

Summary Statement

Designed for rapid deployment by organizations that need to add IT capacity to meet current needs or take advantage of new opportunities, yet lack the space, power, time, and money to use traditional approaches, Product X is the world's first virtualized datacenter, optimized with maximum mobility, and energy, space, and performance efficiency. Housed in a standard 20-foot shipping container, Product X can be deployed anywhere in the world within a matter of weeks – 1/10th the time to deploy a traditional datacenter – at a fraction of the initial cost, with 3x the number of systems in equivalent space and with 20% more efficient cooling/power.

Customer Set:	CIOs who need to quickly ramp datacenter capacity		
Problem/Need	**Value Driver**	**Competitive Positioning**	**Evidence**
A rapidly deployable, more flexible, and less costly datacenter	Mobile datacenters that can be deployed anywhere in 1/10th the time	The world's first virtual, modular datacenter housed in a standard shipping container	Demonstrated density, energy savings, customer testimonials, industry analyst reports

Summary Statement: Only Product X lets you build and deploy a complete datacenter anywhere in the world in 1/10th the time of traditional datacenters, while maximizing space, power and cooling, cutting costs and delivering more capacity per square foot.

Figure 37: Example of a Value Proposition Based on a Real Product

B Integrated Marketing Plan Template

A generic version of the IMP template is available online at:

www.kickstartall.com/campaign_development.html

It is in a Microsoft PowerPoint© template.

Eighty percent of the topics included in this template can be directly applied to your hi-tech marketing model. The trick is in knowing how to customize the remaining 20%.

An approach that works best is to introduce the template as the starting point for your team. Allow them to adapt the template to fit your marketing model. Let them become the author of the final, customized template. Regardless of what your template looks like at the end of the day, the most important thing is that it addresses all the items listed in the table of contents.

Appendix B: Integrated Marketing Plan Template

C The Seven Program Blueprints

Appendix C provides examples of the seven most common types of program blueprints. These blueprint examples are your starting point. They have been kept simple in order to illustrate the connection between the activities and offers. Also notice the story that unfolds in each blueprint example.

Based on your specific marketing model, you many need multiple versions of a single program type. Or, you may find that only a subset of these blueprint types apply to your business. During the course of the synchronization meetings, your team will explore which program themes apply best, and then build from there. They are limited only by your creativity. These blueprints are also available online at:

www.kickstartall.com/campaign_development.html

- Awareness programs (see Figure 38)

- Competitive replacement programs (see Figure 39)

- Cross-sell/up-sell programs (see Figure 40)

- Migration programs (seeFigure 41)

- New customer acquisition programs (see Figure 42)

- Nurture programs (see Figure 43)

- Renewal programs (see Figure 44)

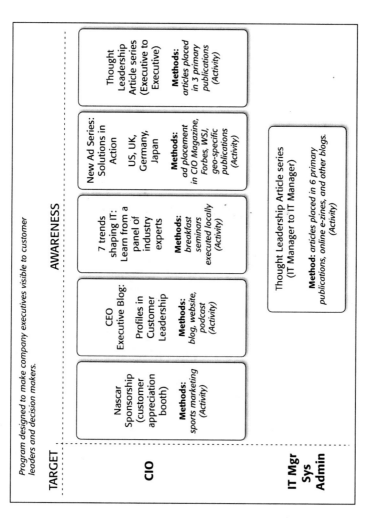

Figure 38: Awareness Program Example: Venues for Thought Leadership

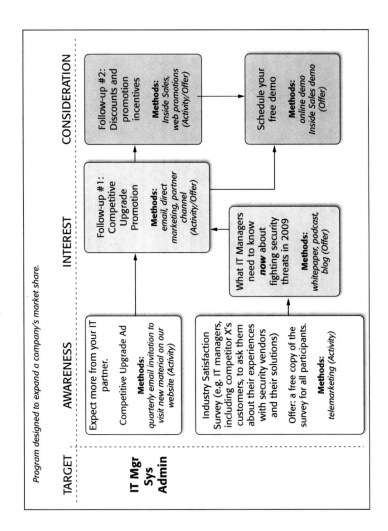

Program designed to expand a company's market share.

TARGET | **AWARENESS** | **INTEREST** | **CONSIDERATION**

IT Mgr Sys Admin

Expect more from your IT partner.

Competitive Upgrade Ad

Methods:
quarterly email invitation to visit new material on our website (Activity)

Industry Satisfaction Survey (e.g. IT managers, including competitor X's customers, to ask them about their experiences with security vendors and their solutions)

Offer: a free copy of the survey for all participants.

Methods:
telemarketing (Activity)

What IT Managers need to know *now* about fighting security threats in 2009

Methods:
whitepaper, podcast, blog (Offer)

Follow-up #1: Competitive Upgrade Promotion

Methods:
email, direct marketing, partner channel (Activity/Offer)

Follow-up #2: Discounts and promotion incentives

Methods:
Inside Sales, web promotions (Activity/Offer)

Schedule your free demo

Methods:
online demo Inside Sales demo (Offer)

Figure 39: Competitive Replacement Program: Unseating a Competitor

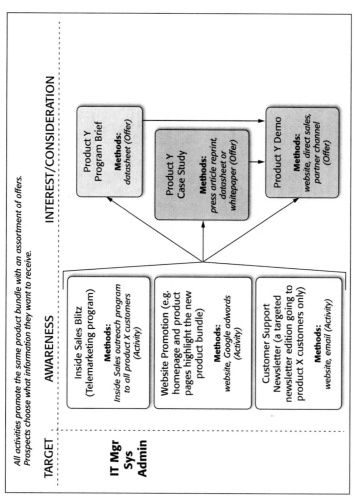

All activities promote the same product bundle with an assortment of offers. Prospects choose what information they want to receive.

TARGET | AWARENESS | INTEREST/CONSIDERATION

IT Mgr
Sys
Admin

Inside Sales Blitz (Telemarketing program)

Methods:
Inside Sales outreach program to all product X customers (Activity)

Website Promotion (e.g. homepage and product pages highlight the new product bundle)

Methods:
website, Google adwords (Activity)

Customer Support Newsletter (a targeted newsletter edition going to product X customers only)

Methods:
website, email (Activity)

Product Y Program Brief

Methods:
datasheet (Offer)

Product Y Case Study

Methods:
press article reprint, datasheet or whitepaper (Offer)

Product Y Demo

Methods:
website, direct sales, partner channel (Offer)

Figure 40: Cross-sell/Up-sell Program: Promoting Product Y to Product X Customers

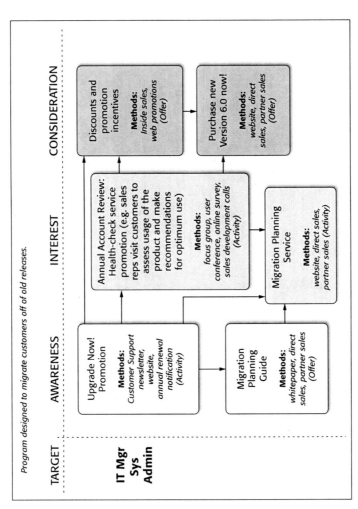

Program designed to migrate customers off of old releases.

TARGET	AWARENESS	INTEREST	CONSIDERATION

IT Mgr Sys Admin

Upgrade Now! Promotion
Methods: *Customer Support newsletter, website, annual renewal notification (Activity)*

Annual Account Review: Health-check service promotion (e.g. sales reps visit customers to assess usage of the product and make recommendations for optimum use)
Methods: *focus group, user conference, online survey, sales development calls (Activity)*

Discounts and promotion incentives
Methods: *Inside sales, web promotions (Offer)*

Migration Planning Guide
Methods: *whitepaper, direct sales, partner sales (Offer)*

Migration Planning Service
Methods: *website, direct sales, partner sales (Activity)*

Purchase new Version 6.0 now!
Methods: *website, direct sales, partner sales (Offer)*

Figure 41: Migration Program Example: Upgrading Customers from Version 5.x to Version 6.0 Program

Appendix C: The Seven Program Blueprints

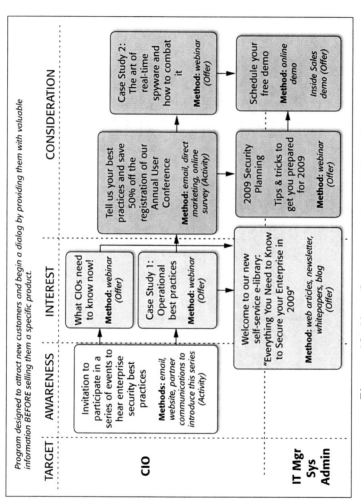

Program designed to attract new customers and begin a dialog by providing them with valuable information BEFORE selling them a specific product.

TARGET	AWARENESS	INTEREST	CONSIDERATION
CIO	Invitation to participate in a series of events to hear enterprise security best practices **Methods:** *email, website, partner communications to introduce this series (Activity)*	What CIOs need to know now! **Method:** *webinar (Offer)* Case Study 1: Operational best practices **Method:** *webinar (Offer)*	Tell us your best practices and save 50% off the registration of our Annual User Conference **Method:** *email, direct marketing, online survey (Activity)* Case Study 2: The art of real-time spyware and how to combat it **Method:** *webinar (Offer)*
IT Mgr Sys Admin		Welcome to our new self-service e-library: "Everything You Need to Know to Secure your Enterprise in 2009" **Method:** *web articles, newsletter, whitepapers, blog (Offer)*	2009 Security Planning Tips & tricks to get you prepared for 2009 **Method:** *webinar (Offer)* Schedule your free demo **Method:** *online demo* *Inside Sales demo (Offer)*

Figure 42: New Customer Acquisition Program

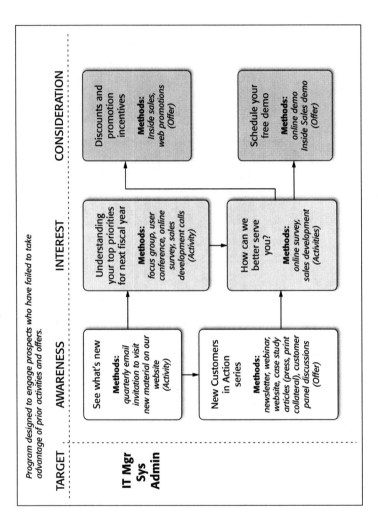

Program designed to engage prospects who have failed to take advantage of prior activities and offers.

TARGET	AWARENESS	INTEREST	CONSIDERATION

**IT Mgr
Sys
Admin**

See what's new

Methods:
*quarterly email invitation to visit new material on our website
(Activity)*

New Customers in Action series

Methods:
*newsletter, webinar, website, case study articles (press, print collateral), customer panel discussions
(Offer)*

Understanding your top priorities for next fiscal year

Methods:
*focus group, user conference, online survey, sales development calls
(Activity)*

How can we better serve you?

Methods:
*online survey, sales development
(Activities)*

Discounts and promotion incentives

Methods:
*Inside sales, web promotions
(Offer)*

Schedule your free demo

Methods:
*online demo
Inside Sales demo
(Offer)*

Figure 43: Nurture Program: Nurturing the Prospect Database

Appendix C: The Seven Program Blueprints

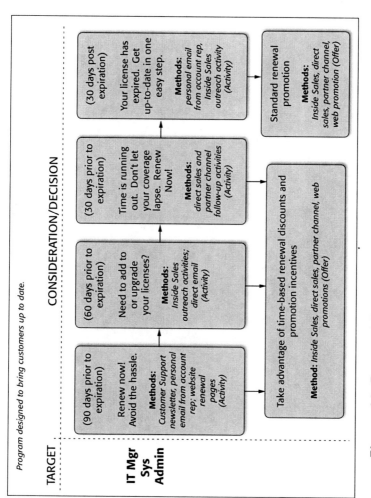

Program designed to bring customers up to date.

TARGET — **CONSIDERATION/DECISION**

IT Mgr
Sys
Admin

(90 days prior to expiration)

Renew now! Avoid the hassle.

Methods:
Customer Support newsletter, personal email from account rep; website renewal pages (Activity)

(60 days prior to expiration)

Need to add to or upgrade your licenses?

Methods:
Inside Sales outreach activities; direct email (Activity)

(30 days prior to expiration)

Time is running out. Don't let your coverage lapse. Renew Now!

Methods:
direct sales and partner channel follow-up activities (Activity)

(30 days post expiration)

Your license has expired. Get up-to-date in one easy step.

Methods:
personal email from account rep, Inside Sales outreach activity (Activity)

Take advantage of time-based renewal discounts and promotion incentives

Method: *Inside Sales, direct sales, partner channel, web promotions (Offer)*

Standard renewal promotion

Methods:
Inside Sales, direct sales, partner channel, web promotion (Offer)

Figure 44: Renewal Program: a License Renewal Program

About the Author

Mike Gospe is a co-founder and principal of KickStart Alliance (www.kickstartall.com), a marketing and sales SWAT team that assists businesses of all sizes in architecting and executing a variety of marketing and sales programs and plans. With more than 20 years of hi-tech marketing experience, Mike is an accomplished leader, marketing strategist and corporate executive, working with marketing leaders to architect and hone their strategies, processes, and plans.

Mike wears the victories and battles scars of campaign development, having worked eight years in the trenches as a campaign manager and then as the director of the campaign management team at both HP and Sun. As a result, Mike was recognized as being one of the key architects that helped these companies reinvent their approach to global integrated marketing planning and execution.

As a recognized leader, Mike has authored a number of marketing- and sales-related articles, and is a frequent guest speaker at venture capitalist and marketing forums on the topics of business and marketing planning, messaging, and sales development. He has a BSEE and an MBA from the University of Santa Clara. Mike and his family live in Los Altos, California.

He can be reached at mikeg@kickstartall.com.

Create Thought Leadership for your Company

Books deliver instant credibility to the author. Having an MBA or PhD is great, however, putting the word "author" in front of your name is similar to using the letters PhD or MBA. You are no long Michael Green, you are "Author Michael Green."

Books give you a platform to stand on. They help you to:

- Demonstrate your thought leadership
- Generate leads

Books deliver increased revenue, particularly indirect revenue

- A typical consultant will make 3x in indirect revenue for every dollar they make on book sales

Books are better than a business card. They are:

- More powerful than white papers
- An item that makes it to the book shelf vs. the circular file
- The best tschocke you can give at a conference

Why wait to write your book?

Check out other companies that have built credibility by writing and publishing a book through Happy About

Contact Happy About at 408-257-3000 or go to http://happyabout.info.

Other Happy About Books

Projects are MESSY!

From the minute the project begins, all manner of changes, surprises and disasters befall them. Unfortunately most of these are PREDICTABLE and AVOIDABLE.

Paperback $19.95
eBook $11.95

Learn the 42 Rules of Marketing!

Compilation of ideas, theories, and practical approaches to marketing challenges that marketers know they should do, but don't always have the time or patience to do.

Paperback $19.95
eBook $11.95

Purchase these books at Happy About
http://happyabout.info or at other online and physical bookstores.

LaVergne, TN USA
17 January 2011
212700LV00004B/114/P